THE BIG CHRISTMAS STORY | FAMILY ADVENT READINGS

Carrien Blue

For Isaiah, Carmina, Sophia, Judah, Ezekiel, and Axl.

I first wrote this book for you. The many Advents I've spent reading to you are some of my fondest memories.

CONTENTS

Light of the World

Most advent meditations focus on the lineage of Jesus and the lives of all the people leading up to him. I love these. We have used them as a family, and will again.

When I wrote this series of meditations I wanted to come at the advent story from a different angle, from a more cosmic perspective that highlights the significance of Jesus coming, and the larger context of Light to the World.

The stories I've selected include many of the people in Jesus lineage, but I've tried to focus on the why of his coming. Why did God choose these people? Why did Jesus have to come?

I don't answer it conclusively of course, that would take a much bigger book. But I hope I have managed to at least point in that direction, to highlight in a few places that ways that God, through history, has been with his people, and the ultimate goal to finally have us become his dwelling place, where his spirit breathes, and his character is known by us in our own hearts.

Take the time to slow down with these. Talk about them. Leave time to think and engage with the story. Please don't tell your children what to think. Let them come to their own conclusions. Ask questions rather than give answers. This is a gentle way to guide your children toward examining many different ways to see and understand this story, and for it to take deep root in their hearts and minds.

Thank you for reading along.

* * *

Carrien Blue

Reading Activities

Thank you for making this meditation a part of your advent celebrations this year. These readings are designed to get your children to engage with the story in a new way and, hopefully, to think about it long after Advent is over.

[Begin with reading 1 on December 1st, reading 2 on December 2nd, etc]

The first year I did these readings with my children it went like this. After the dinner things had been cleared we gathered back at the table, where the Advent wreath remained lit.

Each child had a piece of string tacked up in the dining room with 25 little pieces of paper, numbered 1-25, pinned to it with small clothespins. Each night I handed them the next piece of paper. On the blank side they would draw the things they heard about in the reading. (OR, they drew something else if they were 5 and wanted to do something different. My third child, Sophia began by drawing a nativity scene the first night, the tree and the snake in the garden the second night, and a picture of herself praying on the third night.) What matters is that they have something to do with their little hands while they are listening. Also, that they have a way to count the days.

When the reading is done we pin the paper back up on the string, picture side out, so they have a record of the events in their own retelling. (This may sound complicated, but I promise it's not. I just cut regular white printer paper in quarters and wrote numbers on it with a sharpie. I already had the clothespins and the yarn. I'm sure a craftier more creative mom could use cool paper and cut out numbers and any number of things to make these into Pinterest worthy decorations. Some may even enjoy doing it. Or you can use what you already have and keep it simple. The point is to do it, not to make it perfect.)

Some nights we have special treats to go along with the reading. This is usually on the first night of advent, on Sundays when we add another candle, and when I just feel like giving them dessert. Our treats include: a bit of tea or hot chocolate, a cookie, some eggnog or warm milk. I try to keep it simple. This is the period of waiting after all, not yet of celebration. But I do like to make things cozy. Whatever works for your short people.

We are making memories, and telling one of the greatest biggest stories ever told.

Thank you for reading along. May your waiting be blessed.

If you want include the Advent tradition of lighting candles, and adding another candle each Sunday, I have included a small how-to for you, and additional readings that reflect on each candle's theme. This is optional. You can add it to the daily readings, or skip it, or choose to only read once each Sunday.

All of this is optional. But I hope that if you do it, it will be hope giving and life bringing for you and your family.

I also created coloring pages to go with each reading. Download for free at https://parenting.carrienblue.com/advent-coloring-pages

DECEMBER 1

The Beginning

1 In the beginning God created the heavens and the earth. 2 The earth was formless and void, and darkness was over the surface of the deep, and the Spirit of God was moving over the surface of the waters. 3 Then God said, "Let there be light "; and there was light. (Genesis 1:1-3 NASB)

26 Then God said, "Let Us make man in Our image, according to Our likeness ; and let them rule over the fish of the sea and over the birds of the sky and over the cattle and over all the earth, and over every creeping thing that creeps on the earth."

[7 Then the LORD God formed man of dust from the ground, and breathed into his nostrils the breath of life ; and man became a living being. 8 The LORD God planted a garden toward the east, in Eden ; and there He placed the man whom He had formed.] (Genesis 2:7-8 NASB)

27 God created man in His own image, in the image of God He created him; male and female He created them. 28 God blessed them; and God said to them, "Be fruitful and multiply, and fill the earth, and subdue it; and rule over the fish of the sea and over the birds of the sky and over every living thing that moves on the earth." (Genesis 1:26-28)

The Bible tells us that when God first created the world it was formless and void, or useless and chaotic. But then God spoke. "Let there be light." And there was. There was light in darkness.

* * *

And then God spoke again and brought order to the chaos, and all living things in to being. Finally, he put his own image onto the earth to rule over it.

Who do you think that was?

It was us. He gave us the job of taking care of the earth he made, and he gave us the job of finishing the work he started. Creation wasn't complete when God rested. That's why He made us. **He gave us the important job of completing His work on the earth.** Outside of the garden there was still work to be done. [The language in Hebrew makes this more clear, but the word subdue, is a clue. Subdue means to conquer, to bring under control or rule.] **We were supposed to continue to bring order to the chaos that remained.** We were supposed to continue to bring life and beauty to the earth.

How could we do this?

You see, God made us specially. He did something different with people. He formed man out of the dust of the earth, but then he breathed his own breath into us, **the breath of life.** We had God's own breath in us. God's spirit and power to actually be His image, came with that breath.

Think about the word image for a minute. Do you know what it means?

An image is something that looks like something else, or represents something else. When the Bible says God made us in his image, it means He made us to represent him, **to be His presence here**, on this planet.

It was a big job. But we had everything we needed to do it. We had God with us, close by, and **we had His breath of life in us.**

Prayer: Thank you Father for creating us. Thank you for giving us life and giving our life meaning and purpose by giving us an important job to do. Thank you for making us in your image. Please help us to walk with you, and to breath your breath, and to do our part in completing the creation you began, and fulfilling our mission here on earth.

DECEMBER 2

How We Lost the Breath of Life

1 Now the serpent was more crafty than any beast of the field which the LORD God had made. And he said to the woman, "Indeed , has God said, 'You shall not eat from any tree of the garden '?" 2 The woman said to the serpent, "From the fruit of the trees of the garden we may eat ; 3 but from the fruit of the tree which is in the middle of the garden, God has said, **'You shall not eat from it or touch it, or you will die**.' " 4 The serpent said to the woman, "You surely will not die ! 5 "For God knows that in the day you eat from it your eyes will be opened, and **you will be like God, knowing good and evil**." 6 When the woman saw that the tree was good for food, and that it was a delight to the eyes, and that the tree was desirable to make one wise, she took from its fruit and ate ; and she gave also to her husband with her, and he ate. 7 Then the eyes of both of them were opened, and they knew that they were naked ; and they sewed fig leaves together and made themselves loin coverings. 8 They heard the sound of the LORD God walking in the garden in the cool of the day, and the man and his wife hid themselves from the presence of the LORD God among the trees of the garden. 9 Then the LORD God called to the man, and said to him, "Where are you?" 10 He said, "I heard the sound of You in the garden, and **I was afraid** because I was naked ; so I hid myself." 11 And He said, "Who told you that you were naked ? Have you eaten from

the tree of which I commanded you not to eat ?" 12 The man said, "The woman whom You gave to be with me, she gave me from the tree, and I ate." 13 Then the LORD God said to the woman, "What is this you have done ?" And the woman said, "The serpent deceived me, and I ate."

17 Then to Adam He said, "Because you have listened to the voice of your wife, and have eaten from the tree about which I commanded you, saying, 'You shall not eat from it'; Cursed is the ground because of you; In toil you will eat of it All the days of your life. 18 "Both thorns and thistles it shall grow for you; And you will eat the plants of the field ; 19 By the sweat of your face You will eat bread, Till you return to the ground, Because from it you were taken ; **For you are dust, And to dust you shall return.**" 20 Now the man called his wife's name Eve, because she was the mother of all the living. 21 The LORD God made garments of skin for Adam and his wife, and clothed them. 22 Then the LORD God said, "Behold, the man has become like one of Us, knowing good and evil ; and now, he might stretch out his hand, and take also from the tree of life, and eat, and live forever "- 23 therefore the LORD God sent him out from the garden of Eden, to cultivate the ground from which he was taken. (Genesis 3:1-13,17-23 NASB - emphasis mine)

Wait, what?

What just happened?

How did the first humans go from having the Breath of Life in them, and the power to complete creation and to be God's presence on the earth to being nothing but dust again, toiling away in dust and returning to dust when they die? [This question isn't rhetorical. This is an opportunity for kids to narrate back the story they just heard, for practice in retention, and so you can hear from their lips what they heard and understood.]

* * *

Did Adam and Eve die when they ate the fruit, like God said?

Well, they could still talk and walk around it looks like. But **some very important things changed**. What were those things?

For starters, they felt ashamed. **Suddenly they looked at themselves, and felt like something was wrong with them.** So they tried to fix it themselves by covering themselves up to hide what was wrong.

They were afraid of God. **They had never been afraid of God before**. They had always talked to him and known he loved them. Now they hid from him. They didn't want him to see what was wrong with them. They knew now that something was wrong, and they didn't want him to see.

How sad!

But God knows that something has gone wrong. He knows that they shouldn't be afraid, or ashamed. And he knows how it happened too.

Eve wanted to impress God, or be more special, by knowing about good and evil, instead of just trusting God, instead of just breathing his breath. **She wanted to breath on her own**, and there was no life there. Now she and Adam are stuck with the knowledge of good and evil and no life, and the earth is changed because of it. Think about how much power God must have given them for their choice to change the earth as significantly as it did. Because they didn't obey, the ground was cursed, thorns and thistles grew out of it, and because they lost the Breath of Life, everything was going to be hard for them to do now. Just surviving was going to be hard.

Not only that, but **now they would know death**. They would go back to the dust God made them from. God had to send them out of the garden. **Everything had changed.**

How do you think God felt about all of this? Can you tell from the story?

How do you think he felt about Adam and Eve?

* * *

Let's look at what he does. He calls for them. He looks for them. Then he tells them the full weight of what they did, and what will happen because of it. But **he doesn't abandon them there.** He gives them clothes of animal skin and **sends them out of the garden into the world they were meant to rule, to make it as best they can.**

But this isn't the end of the story, thankfully. Because **God is going to find a way to put his breath back into us.** This is the story of advent. This is the story of the whole Bible, how God is going to get the Breath of Life back into people.

Prayer: Father God, please help us to trust in you. Thank you that you never abandon us, even when we disobey. Help us to remember that you give us life and you want only good for us. When we are tempted to blame others for our poor choices, help us to take responsibility for our own actions. Help us to go to you, even if we are afraid because we know that we have disobeyed. Thank you that you always love us.

DECEMBER 3

Abraham - The Beginning of God's Plan

1 Now the LORD said to Abram, "Go forth from your country, And from your relatives And from your father's house, To the land which I will show you; 2 And I will make you a great nation, And I will bless you, And make your name great ; And so you shall be a blessing ; 3 And I will bless those who bless you, And the one who curses you I will curse. And in you all the families of the earth will be blessed." 4 So Abram went forth as the LORD had spoken to him; and Lot went with him. Now Abram was seventy-five years old when he departed from Haran. 5 Abram took Sarai his wife and Lot his nephew , and all their possessions which they had accumulated, and the persons which they had acquired in Haran, and they set out for the land of Canaan ; thus they came to the land of Canaan. 6 Abram passed through the land as far as the site of Shechem, to the oak of Moreh. Now the Canaanite was then in the land. 7 The LORD appeared to Abram and said, "To your descendants I will give this land." So he built an altar there to the LORD who had appeared to him. 8 Then he proceeded from there to the mountain on the east of Bethel, and pitched his tent, with Bethel on the west and Ai on the east ; and there he built an altar to the LORD and called upon the name of the LORD. (Genesis 11:1-8 NASB)

1 Now when Abram was ninety-nine years old, the LORD appeared to Abram and said to him, "I am

God Almighty ; Walk before Me, and be blameless. 2 "I will establish My covenant between Me and you, And I will multiply you exceedingly." 3 Abram fell on his face, and God talked with him, saying, 4 "As for Me, behold, My covenant is with you, And you will be the father of a multitude of nations. 5 "No longer shall your name be called Abram, But your name shall be Abraham ; For I will make you the father of a multitude of nations. 6 "I will make you exceedingly fruitful, and I will make nations of you, and kings will come forth from you. 7 "I will establish My covenant between Me and you and your descendants after you throughout their generations for an everlasting covenant, to be God to you and to your descendants after you. 8 "I will give to you and to your descendants after you, the land of your sojournings, all the land of Canaan, for an everlasting possession ; and I will be their God." (Genesis 17:1-8 NASB)

A lot happens on earth between when Adam and Eve leave the garden and God starts talking to this guy named Abram. He's had a lot of time to see how people do on their own. It hasn't turned out very well. They get into all sorts of trouble.

So God tells this guy Abram, somehow, to leave home, take all his stuff with him, and God will give him a new land and make him into a great nation. Now it doesn't tell us exactly how God tells all this stuff to Abram, but it must have been convincing. Abram packs up his wife and his nephew, and all his stuff, including servants, and leaves behind everything he has ever known in order to follow this God he doesn't know into the wild blue yonder.

Some people talk about Abram having great faith at this point. Maybe that's true. Or maybe, the promise of a new land, being a great nation and being able to bless and curse whomever he liked sounded like a pretty sweet deal. Maybe that's why he went. It probably didn't matter to God why. Because God doesn't need perfect people, he just needs willing people. He's pretty good at filling in the blanks. Even when, like Abram, you are a total coward sometimes and make a mess of things because you are afraid and you lose faith and try to do things your own way. God can still work with that.

God even appears to Abram many times. It's so amazing that he Abram falls on his face. God hasn't appeared to very many people since Adam and Eve left the garden, though it has happened. But God is still there, with people, and talking to those who will listen.

But why does God call Abram? What's his plan?

He says that through his descendants all the earth will be blessed. What does that mean?

He also says that he will make a covenant with Abraham's descendants and that he will be their God and he will be there for them and keep his promises to them. (Notice how God changes Abram's name also.)

It's obvious that God has a plan. Something big is going to happen. If you don't know what it is yet, you'll just have to keep reading in order to find out. What are your guesses?

Prayer: God of Abraham, God with a plan, thank you. Thank you that you don't need us to be perfect, or brave, to be able to invite us to walk with you into something new. Thank you that it is enough to take that first step and trust you to guide us. Help us remember that you can work with us, where we are at, and that we can start right now to let you guide us and walk with you. Thank you that life with you is so much bigger and more amazing than it would be if we tried to do things our own way.

DECEMBER 4

Sarah, Part of God's Plan Too

1 Now Sarai, Abram's wife had borne him no children, and she had an Egyptian maid whose name was Hagar. 2 So Sarai said to Abram, "Now behold, the LORD has prevented me from bearing children. Please go in to my maid ; perhaps I will obtain children through her." And Abram listened to the voice of Sarai. 3 After Abram had lived ten years in the land of Canaan, Abram's wife Sarai took Hagar the Egyptian, her maid, and gave her to her husband Abram as his wife. 4 He went in to Hagar, and she conceived; ... 15 So Hagar bore Abram a son ; and Abram called the name of his son, whom Hagar bore, Ishmael. 16 Abram was eighty-six years old when Hagar bore Ishmael to him." (Genesis 16:1-4, 15-16 NASB)

1 Now the LORD appeared to him by the oaks of Mamre, while he was sitting at the tent door in the heat of the day. 2 When he lifted up his eyes and looked, behold, three men were standing opposite him; and when he saw them, he ran from the tent door to meet them and bowed himself to the earth, 3 and said, "My Lord, if now I have found favor in Your sight, please do not pass your servant by. 4 "Please let a little water be brought and wash your feet, and rest yourselves under the tree ; 5 and I will bring a piece of bread, that you may refresh yourselves ; after that you may go on, since you have visited your servant." And they said, "So do, as you

have said." 6 So Abraham hurried into the tent to Sarah, and said, "Quickly, prepare three measures of fine flour , knead it and make bread cakes." 7 Abraham also ran to the herd, and took a tender and choice calf and gave it to the servant, and he hurried to prepare it. 8 He took curds and milk and the calf which he had prepared, and placed it before them; and he was standing by them under the tree as they ate. 9 Then they said to him, "Where is Sarah your wife ?" And he said, "There, in the tent." 10 He said, "I will surely return to you at this time next year ; and behold, Sarah your wife will have a son." And Sarah was listening at the tent door, which was behind him. 11 Now Abraham and Sarah were old, advanced in age ; Sarah was past childbearing . 12 Sarah laughed to herself, saying, "After I have become old, shall I have pleasure, my lord being old also?" 13 And the LORD said to Abraham, "Why did Sarah laugh, saying, 'Shall I indeed bear a child, when I am so old ?' 14 "Is anything too difficult for the LORD ? At the appointed time I will return to you, at this time next year, and Sarah will have a son." 15 Sarah denied it however, saying, "I did not laugh "; for she was afraid. And He said, "No, but you did laugh." (Genesis 18:1-15)

1 Then the LORD took note of Sarah as He had said, and the LORD did for Sarah as He had promised. 2 So Sarah conceived and bore a son to Abraham in his old age, at the appointed time of which God had spoken to him. 3 Abraham called the name of his son who was born to him, whom Sarah bore to him, Isaac. ... 5 Now Abraham was one hundred years old when his son Isaac was born to him. 6 Sarah said, "God has made laughter for me; everyone who hears will laugh with me." 7 And she said, "Who would have said to Abraham that Sarah would nurse children ? Yet I have borne him a son in his old age." (Genesis 21:1-3, 5-7 NASB)

There were a couple of problems with this plan that God had. At least, from Abraham and Sarah's perspective there were. The question they continued to ask, for more than a decade after they followed God to Canaan was, "How is Abraham going to be the father of many nations if his wife couldn't even have one child?"

They were old, and getting older, and there had been no baby for them. As time goes by Sarah gets it into her head that maybe she isn't intended to be part of fulfilling the promise. Maybe, for God to keep his promise to Abraham, she needs to get out of the way. Maybe another woman was supposed to bear the promise and give Abraham children. Abraham thinks she might be right, so he takes Hagar as a wife too. (You could do that kind of thing back in those days. It wasn't as weird as it would be now.) Hagar does bear Abraham a son. He's not the son God had planned, but God takes care of her and Ishmael anyway and blesses them.

But God has his own plans, and Sarah, the one who thinks it's impossible for her to be a part of them herself, figures right into the center of it. She laughs to hear the promise delivered because the thought is too ridiculous. But you will find, as we go through this story, that God often chooses the most unlikely people to accomplish his plans. **It's not ridiculous at all that someone like you, or me, or even Sarah could be part of God's plan for healing the world, and finishing the work.**

The things that seem hard to us aren't hard for God at all.

Can you list all the reasons that Sarah had to believe that it was impossible for her to have a baby?

She had never had a baby, even when she was young. She couldn't have babies. Something was wrong in her body.

She was very old now, too old to have children even if everything worked properly. Her husband was very old now too, almost 100! He was too old to father children.

Sarah had good reasons to laugh, and to doubt.

But God gave her a baby anyway. A little boy named Isaac, which means laughter. Now Isaac too was part of God's plan to bless all of the earth. He was the way that God would keep his promise to Abraham.

Prayer: Thank you God that even when we think that we aren't meant to be a part of your promise, when we think it's impossible, you make a way. Thank you that you bring us all into your big story, your big plan to redeem and heal the earth. You make room for all of us in your family. Help us to trust you to accomplish the promises you have made, and to be open to how you will include us in your plan, and in your promises.

DECEMBER 5

Isaac, The Miracle Child

1 Now it came about after these things, that God tested Abraham, and said to him, "Abraham !" And he said, "Here I am." 2 He said, "Take now your son, your only son, whom you love, Isaac, and go to the land of Moriah, and offer him there as a burnt offering on one of the mountains of which I will tell you." 3 So Abraham rose early in the morning and saddled his donkey, and took two of his young men with him and Isaac his son ; and he split wood for the burnt offering, and arose and went to the place of which God had told him. 4 On the third day Abraham raised his eyes and saw the place from a distance. 5 Abraham said to his young men, "Stay here with the donkey, and I and the lad will go over there ; and we will worship and return to you." 6 Abraham took the wood of the burnt offering and laid it on Isaac his son, and he took in his hand the fire and the knife. So the two of them walked on together. 7 Isaac spoke to Abraham his father and said, "My father !" And he said, "Here I am, my son." And he said, "Behold, the fire and the wood, but where is the lamb for the burnt offering ?" 8 Abraham said, "God will provide for Himself the lamb for the burnt offering, my son." So the two of them walked on together. 9 Then they came to the place of which God had told him; and Abraham built the altar there and arranged the wood, and bound his son Isaac and laid him on the altar, on top of the wood. 10 Abraham

stretched out his hand and took the knife to slay his son. 11 But the angel of the LORD called to him from heaven and said, "Abraham, Abraham !" And he said, "Here I am." 12 He said, "Do not stretch out your hand against the lad, and do nothing to him; for now I know that you fear God, since you have not withheld your son, your only son, from Me." 13 Then Abraham raised his eyes and looked, and behold, behind him a ram caught in the thicket by his horns ; and Abraham went and took the ram and offered him up for a burnt offering in the place of his son. 14 Abraham called the name of that place The LORD Will Provide, as it is said to this day, "In the mount of the LORD it will be provided." 15 Then the angel of the LORD called to Abraham a second time from heaven, 16 and said, "By Myself I have sworn, declares the LORD, because you have done this thing and have not withheld your son, your only son, 17 indeed I will greatly bless you, and I will greatly multiply your seed as the stars of the heavens and as the sand which is on the seashore ; and your seed shall possess the gate of their enemies. 18 "In your seed all the nations of the earth shall be blessed, because you have obeyed My voice." (Genesis 22:1-18 NASB)

Isaac was the impossible child. He was the one promised by God, born to an impossibly old mother, and an impossibly old father and he was a miracle.

So why on earth would God tell Abraham to take this miracle boy up on a mountain and offer him as a sacrifice to God?

It seems sort of mean, doesn't it? How would you like it if your mom and dad gave you something that you really, really wanted, and you were so happy and then one day asked you to give i back to them as a gift? How would you feel about that?

Would you care more about the gift that they gave you, or them, the ones who love you and gave you the gift in the first place?

* * *

Would it be a hard choice for you?

For Abraham it must have been so hard! This wasn't just a thing. This was his son, whom he loved so much.

But you know, Abraham had been walking with God for many years at this time. He had seen some pretty amazing things, including the way God had given him Isaac. It tells us in the book of Hebrews (11:19) that as he walked up that mountain with Isaac "He considered that God is able to raise people even from the dead". Abraham was so sure at this point that God would keep his promise to him that he expected that God would just do another miracle, and give Isaac back to him again. That's a lot of trust.

He was right though. God did give Isaac back to him again. He was right to trust God.

Abraham has learned a lot in the years he has been following God, and he has seen that God keeps promises, and cares about him, and everyone with him.

God's plan to show people who He is, starting with Abraham, is working. Abraham knows now that he can always trust God, and he will teach his descendants the same.

Prayer: God who provides, thank you that trusting in you is never a mistake. Thank you that even as you ask us to choose obedience, and put everything you give us on the line, you are ready and able to provide what we need in order to obey you. Please help us to trust and obey you, even when it makes no sense, even when it's hard. It is only when we step forward in faith that we experience your provision.

DECEMBER 6

Jacob Meets God

21 Isaac prayed to the LORD on behalf of his wife, because she was barren ; and the LORD answered him and Rebekah his wife conceived. 22 But the children struggled together within her; and she said, "If it is so, why then am I this way?" So she went to inquire of the LORD. 23 The LORD said to her, "Two nations are in your womb ; And two peoples will be separated from your body ; And one people shall be stronger than the other ; And the older shall serve the younger." 24 When her days to be delivered were fulfilled, behold, there were twins in her womb. 25 Now the first came forth red, all over like a hairy garment ; and they named him Esau. 26 Afterward his brother came forth with his hand holding on to Esau's heel, so his name was called Jacob ;(Genesis 25:21-26 NASB)

19 Jacob said to his father, "I am Esau your firstborn ; I have done as you told me. Get up, please, sit and eat of my game, that you may bless me." 20 Isaac said to his son, "How is it that you have it so quickly, my son ?" And he said, "Because the LORD your God caused it to happen to me." ... he blessed him and said, "See, the smell of my son Is like the smell of a field which the LORD has blessed ; 28 Now may God give you of the dew of heaven, And of the fatness of the earth, And an abundance of grain and new wine ; 29 May peoples serve you, And nations bow down to you; Be master of your brothers, And

may your mother's sons bow down to you. Cursed be
those who curse you, And blessed be those who bless
you."

When Isaac got old, he decided to give his final blessing to Esau, his
older son. Jacob had already bargained Esau out of his inheritance,
trading it with him for a bowl of stew when he was hungry. In this part
of the story, following his mother's instructions, Jacob pretends to be
Esau, disguising himself and taking food into his old father who can't
see any more. Isaac gives Jacob the blessing that we had planned to
give to Esau, and Esau is angry and heartbroken.

30 Now it came about, as soon as Isaac had finished
blessing Jacob, and Jacob had hardly gone out from
the presence of Isaac his father, that Esau his brother
came in from his hunting. 31 Then he also made
savory food, and brought it to his father ; and he said
to his father, "Let my father arise and eat of his son's
game, that you may bless me." 32 Isaac his father said
to him, "Who are you?" And he said, "I am your son,
your firstborn, Esau." 33 Then Isaac trembled
violently , and said, "Who was he then that hunted
game and brought it to me, so that I ate of all of it
before you came, and blessed him? Yes, and he shall
be blessed." 34 When Esau heard the words of his
father, he cried out with an exceedingly great and
bitter cry, and said to his father, "Bless me, even me
also, O my father !" 35 And he said, "Your brother
came deceitfully and has taken away your blessing."
36 Then he said, "Is he not rightly named Jacob, for he
has supplanted me these two times ? He took away
my birthright, and behold, now he has taken away
my blessing." And he said, "Have you not reserved a
blessing for me?" 37 But Isaac replied to Esau,
"Behold, I have made him your master, and all his
relatives I have given to him as servants ; and with
grain and new wine I have sustained him. Now as for
you then, what can I do, my son ?" 38 Esau said to his
father, "Do you have only one blessing, my father ?
Bless me, even me also, O my father." So Esau lifted

his voice and wept. 39 Then Isaac his father answered and said to him, "Behold, away from the fertility of the earth shall be your dwelling, And away from the dew of heaven from above. 40 "By your sword you shall live, And your brother you shall serve ; But it shall come about when you become restless, That you will break his yoke from your neck." 41 So Esau bore a grudge against Jacob because of the blessing with which his father had blessed him; and Esau said to himself, "The days of mourning for my father are near ; then I will kill my brother Jacob." 42 Now when the words of her elder son Esau were reported to Rebekah, she sent and called her younger son Jacob, and said to him, "Behold your brother Esau is consoling himself concerning you by planning to kill you. 43 "Now therefore, my son, obey my voice, and arise, flee to Haran, to my brother Laban ! 44 "Stay with him a few days, until your brother's fury subsides, 45 until your brother's anger against you subsides and he forgets what you did to him.

10 Then Jacob departed from Beersheba and went toward Haran. 11 He came to a certain place and spent the night there, because the sun had set ; and he took one of the stones of the place and put it under his head, and lay down in that place. 12 He had a dream, and behold, a ladder was set on the earth with its top reaching to heaven ; and behold, the angels of God were ascending and descending on it. 13 And behold, the LORD stood above it and said, "I am the LORD, the God of your father Abraham and the God of Isaac ; the land on which you lie, I will give it to you and to your descendants. 14 "Your descendants will also be like the dust of the earth, and you will spread out to the west and to the east and to the north and to the south ; and in you and in your descendants shall all the families of the earth be blessed. 15 "Behold, I am with you and will keep you wherever you go, and will bring you back to this land ; for I will not leave you until I have done what I have promised you." 16 Then Jacob awoke from his

sleep and said, "Surely the LORD is in this place, and I did not know it." 17 He was afraid and said, "How awesome is this place ! This is none other than the house of God, and this is the gate of heaven." 18 So Jacob rose early in the morning, and took the stone that he had put under his head and set it up as a pillar and poured oil on its top. 19 He called the name of that place Bethel ; however, previously the name of the city had been Luz. 20 Then Jacob made a vow, saying, "If God will be with me and will keep me on this journey that I take, and will give me food to eat and garments to wear, 21 and I return to my father's house in safety, then the LORD will be my God. 22 "This stone, which I have set up as a pillar, will be God's house, and of all that You give me I will surely give a tenth to You." (Genesis 28:10-22 NASB)

What can we say about Jacob, Isaac's second born son? He's not exactly the kind of guy who is a good role model, that's for sure. He steals from his brother, he tricks his father. Now he is running away, because his brother is so angry at him that he wants to kill him. You can't really blame him either. Jacob just took everything away from Esau, everything that mattered to him anyway.

It seems a pretty odd moment for God to appear to him and say, "I am with you, I will keep you wherever you go, and will bring you back to this land; for I will not leave you until I have done what I have promised you."

Do you think Jacob deserved God's blessing?

Jacob has just received the same promise from God that Abraham did. He is obviously God's choice for his plan to continue. Once again, God is choosing an unlikely person, the younger and weaker brother who is a cheater a liar and a thief. He's choosing a person who isn't exactly special and he promises him amazing things. He show's himself to Jacob and blesses him.

Why do you think that is?

* * *

31

It appears God doesn't choose people based on who is the most good, or pretty, or strong. He can use anyone it seems. They just have to say yes.

But something happens to Jacob after this meeting with God. He starts to change. God takes care of him as He promised, and Jacob also learns to trust God, and becomes a different kind of man by the end.

Prayer: Thank you God that you choose us. You don't wait for us to choose you, from the beginning you have chosen us, and you are always with us, even when we don't know it. Thank you that your love for us doesn't depend on how we behave. Your love is constant and unchanging. Help us to do as Jacob did, to turn toward you and choose you in the moment when you show yourself to us.

DECEMBER 7

How God Redeems

18 When they [Israel's sons] saw him [Joseph] from a
distance and before he came close to them, they
plotted against him to put him to death. 19 They said
to one another, "Here comes this dreamer ! 20 "Now
then, come and let us kill him and throw him into one
of the pits ; and we will say, 'A wild beast devoured
him.' Then let us see what will become of his
dreams !" 21 But Reuben heard this and rescued him
out of their hands and said, "Let us not take his life."
22 Reuben further said to them, "Shed no blood.
Throw him into this pit that is in the wilderness, but
do not lay hands on him"-that he might rescue him
out of their hands, to restore him to his father. 23 So it
came about, when Joseph reached his brothers, that
they stripped Joseph of his tunic, the varicolored
tunic that was on him; 24 and they took him and
threw him into the pit. Now the pit was empty,
without any water in it. 25 Then they sat down to eat
a meal. And as they raised their eyes and looked,
behold, a caravan of Ishmaelites was coming from
Gilead, with their camels bearing aromatic gum and
balm and myrrh, on their way to bring them down to
Egypt. 26 Judah said to his brothers, "What profit is it
for us to kill our brother and cover up his blood ? 27
"Come and let us sell him to the Ishmaelites and not
lay our hands on him, for he is our brother, our own
flesh." And his brothers listened to him. 28 Then
some Midianite traders passed by, so they pulled him

up and lifted Joseph out of the pit, and sold him to the Ishmaelites for twenty shekels of silver. Thus they brought Joseph into Egypt. 29 Now Reuben returned to the pit, and behold, Joseph was not in the pit ; so he tore his garments. 30 He returned to his brothers and said, "The boy is not there; as for me, where am I to go ?" 31 So they took Joseph's tunic, and slaughtered a male goat and dipped the tunic in the blood ; 32 and they sent the varicolored tunic and brought it to their father and said, "We found this ; please examine it to see whether it is your son's tunic or not." 33 Then he examined it and said, "It is my son's tunic. A wild beast has devoured him; Joseph has surely been torn to pieces !" 34 So Jacob tore his clothes, and put sackcloth on his loins and mourned for his son many days. 35 Then all his sons and all his daughters arose to comfort him, but he refused to be comforted. And he said, "Surely I will go down to Sheol in mourning for my son." So his father wept for him. 36 Meanwhile, the Midianites sold him in Egypt to Potiphar, Pharaoh's officer, the captain of the bodyguard. (Genesis 37:18-36 NASB)

1 Then Joseph could not control himself before all those who stood by him, and he cried, "Have everyone go out from me." So there was no man with him when Joseph made himself known to his brothers. 2 He wept so loudly that the Egyptians heard it, and the household of Pharaoh heard of it. 3 Then Joseph said to his brothers, "I am Joseph ! Is my father still alive ?" But his brothers could not answer him, for they were dismayed at his presence. 4 Then Joseph said to his brothers, "Please come closer to me." And they came closer. And he said, "I am your brother Joseph, whom you sold into Egypt. 5 "Now do not be grieved or angry with yourselves, because you sold me here, for God sent me before you to preserve life. 6 "For the famine has been in the land these two years, and there are still five years in which there will be neither plowing nor harvesting. 7 "God sent me before you to preserve for you a remnant in

the earth, and to keep you alive by a great deliverance. 8 "Now, therefore, it was not you who sent me here, but God ; and He has made me a father to Pharaoh and lord of all his household and ruler over all the land of Egypt. 9 "Hurry and go up to my father, and say to him, 'Thus says your son Joseph, "God has made me lord of all Egypt ; come down to me, do not delay. 10 "You shall live in the land of Goshen, and you shall be near me, you and your children and your children's children and your flocks and your herds and all that you have. 11 "There I will also provide for you, for there are still five years of famine to come, and you and your household and all that you have would be impoverished.'" (Genesis 45:1-11 NASB)

Do you remember Jacob, and the vision he had of the ladder going up into heaven? Well, God has since changed his name to Israel, and he has 12 sons! His favorite son is Joseph. He gives Joseph special treatment, a multicolored coat, and keeps him close beside him while he sends the other boys to tend the flocks.

How do you think the other boys felt about that?

Special treatment might have been ok, but then God starts sending Joseph dreams that can only mean that one day his brothers will all bow down to him, and he won't stop talking about them. This makes the brothers so angry that they plot to get rid of Joseph for good. Only because of Reuben do they change their mind about killing him. Instead, they sell him to slave traders while Reuben is gone, so they can make some money off of him.

This is a terrible story. Can you imagine how Joseph feels, to be sold as a slave by his brothers because they hate him so much?

How do you think the brothers felt once they saw how very sad their father was?

You may have noticed that these stories have a lot of people in them that do very wrong things. These people that God has put himself into the story with, they aren't all that good.

Now Joseph is a slave in Egypt, for years, and for more years after that he's in prison in Egypt and it seems that his story can't get any worse. Back at home his brothers are living with the guilt of what they did, and the grief they caused their father and there is no way to fix it. None.

But God...

Well, God is in the business of fixing, of lighting the way when things are at their darkest, of using our very worst moments as the very way he will bring about something wonderful. That's what redemption is, and God is very good at it.

God has taken Abraham from a coward of a man with no children to a man of great faith who's children and grandchildren will cover the earth. He's turned Jacob from a liar and a cheat into a man who acts honorably, who walks with God, and at the end of his life can see far enough ahead to know which of Joseph's sons descendants God will bring the promised blessing through.

Now he turns Joseph's captivity into blessing. Joseph becomes a ruler in Egypt, with the ability to care for and provide for his father's family, and bring them to a place where they can grow into a great nation.

Not only that, but he gives Joseph the strength to forgive his brothers, when he has the power to destroy them. He gives Joseph's brothers another chance to do the right thing, to mend what they have broken. He brings a family torn apart back together.

Do you think you would forgive, if you were Joseph? How do you think his brothers felt once they found out he was alive?

Can you think of anything in your own life that feels like it's hopeless, and there is no way it can be fixed? Do you think maybe God, who redeemed this situation for Joseph, might be able to do something about yours?

* * *

Prayer: God who redeems, who turns evil for good, who brings reconciliation and forgiveness in families, help us to forgive. Help us to trust you in the dark, until we see the light. Help us to remember that you are always working to write a beautiful ending to our messy sad stories.

DECEMBER 8

The Slaves Are Freed

1 Now Moses was pasturing the flock of Jethro his father-in-law, the priest of Midian ; and he led the flock to the west side of the wilderness and came to Horeb, the mountain of God. 2 The angel of the LORD appeared to him in a blazing fire from the midst of a bush ; and he looked, and behold, the bush was burning with fire, yet the bush was not consumed. 3 So Moses said, "I must turn aside now and see this marvelous sight, why the bush is not burned up." 4 When the LORD saw that he turned aside to look, God called to him from the midst of the bush and said, "Moses, Moses !" And he said, "Here I am." 5 Then He said, "Do not come near here ; remove your sandals from your feet, for the place on which you are standing is holy ground." 6 He said also, "I am the God of your father, the God of Abraham, the God of Isaac, and the God of Jacob." Then Moses hid his face, for he was afraid to look at God. 7 The LORD said, "I have surely seen the affliction of My people who are in Egypt, and have given heed to their cry because of their taskmasters, for I am aware of their sufferings. 8 "So I have come down to deliver them from the power of the Egyptians, and to bring them up from that land to a good and spacious land, to a land flowing with milk and honey, to the place of the Canaanite and the Hittite and the Amorite and the Perizzite and the Hivite and the Jebusite. 9 "Now, behold, the cry of the

sons of Israel has come to Me; furthermore, I have seen the oppression with which the Egyptians are oppressing them. 10 "Therefore, come now, and I will send you to Pharaoh, so that you may bring My people, the sons of Israel, out of Egypt." 11 But Moses said to God, **"Who am I, that I should go to Pharaoh, and that I should bring the sons of Israel out of Egypt ?"** 12 And He said, "Certainly I will be with you, and this shall be the sign to you that it is I who have sent you: when you have brought the people out of Egypt, you shall worship God at this mountain." (Exodus 3:1-12)

The Israelites, that is, all the descendants of Israel and his sons, have been living in Egypt for hundreds of years now, and they have grown very strong. They are so strong that pharaoh is worried that they may be a threat to Egypt. So he starts to do really bad things to try and make them weaker. He tries to get rid of all the baby boys, so there won't be any boys who can fight against Egypt. He makes slaves of all the people of Israel, forcing them to make bricks for his massive building projects, and the people cry out to God for him to help them.

Moses is one of the baby boys that Pharaoh tried to get rid of. Now he is a grown man living in the desert, and God calls him and tells him to go to Egypt and tell Pharaoh to let his people go.

Moses doesn't sound too happy about this assignment, does he?

Moses doesn't think he should be the one that God chooses to set Israel free. But God promises Moses, as he has promised Abraham, Isaac, and Jacob before him, that he will be with him, and that he will return, with all of Israel to this mountain to again meet with God.

Do you know the rest of this story?

Does God keep his promise?

Does Moses bring all the tribes of Israel out of Egypt and back to Mt. Sinai?

* * *

It's a very exciting story, and you can read more about it if you like in Exodus, starting at chapter 1.

Tomorrow we'll find out if they make it to Sinai or not.

Prayer: God who sees the ones who are suffering, thank you. Thank you that you see injustice, that you free those who are oppressed. Help us to be the ones who cry out to you for justice, the ones who help the oppressed. Help us as your people to be the ones who rescue the helpless. Instead of asking "Who am I to do this thing?" Help us to ask you, "What would you have me do?"

DECEMBER 9

Meeting God Face to Face

1 In the third month after the sons of Israel had gone out of the land of Egypt, on that very day they came into the wilderness of Sinai. 2 When they set out from Rephidim, they came to the wilderness of Sinai and camped in the wilderness ; and there Israel camped in front of the mountain. 3 Moses went up to God, and the LORD called to him from the mountain, saying, "Thus you shall say to the house of Jacob and tell the sons of Israel : 4 'You yourselves have seen what I did to the Egyptians, and how I bore you on eagles' wings, and brought you to Myself. 5 'Now then, if you will indeed obey My voice and keep My covenant, then you shall be My own possession among all the peoples, for all the earth is Mine; 6 and you shall be to Me a kingdom of priests and a holy nation.' These are the words that you shall speak to the sons of Israel." 7 So Moses came and called the elders of the people, and set before them all these words which the LORD had commanded him. 8 All the people answered together and said, "All that the LORD has spoken we will do !" And Moses brought back the words of the people to the LORD. 9 The LORD said to Moses, "Behold, I will come to you in a thick cloud, so that the people may hear when I speak with you and may also believe in you forever."

16 So it came about on the third day, when it was morning, that there were thunder and lightning flashes and a thick cloud upon the mountain and a

very loud trumpet sound, so that all the people who were in the camp trembled. 17 And Moses brought the people out of the camp to meet God, and they stood at the foot of the mountain. 18 Now Mount Sinai was all in smoke because the LORD descended upon it in fire ; and its smoke ascended like the smoke of a furnace, and the whole mountain quaked violently. 19 When the sound of the trumpet grew louder and louder, Moses spoke and God answered him with thunder. 20 The LORD came down on Mount Sinai, to the top of the mountain ; and the LORD called Moses to the top of the mountain, and Moses went up. (Exodus 19:1-20 NASB)

18 All the people perceived the thunder and the lightning flashes and the sound of the trumpet and the mountain smoking ; and when the people saw it, they trembled and stood at a distance. 19 Then they said to Moses, "Speak to us yourself and we will listen ; but let not God speak to us, or we will die." (Exodus 20:18-19 NASB)

God has done mighty wonders, and crushed the strength of Egypt, and brought Israel safely back to the place where he first appeared to Moses in the burning bush so that they all can meet with him. He plans to stay with this people, to be right in the midst of them and make them into a holy nation, where all of them can be in the presence of God.

How do the people react when God comes down on the mountain to meet with them?

Do they want God to talk to them directly?

Do you think you would be scared if God came to talk to you and the earth shook, and there was lightening, smoke, and fire, and the sounds of trumpets blowing all at once?

God does stay with his people in the wilderness, and guide them himself to the land where promised he would take them, the land he promised to Abraham, Isaac and Jacob. But he only talks to Moses. The rest of the people don't want to hear God's voice directly. It's too scary for them.

A long time later though the prophets begin to tell of a time when God will come and live with his people again, and this time they will hear him. This first time that God comes to his people it is with fire and smoke and trumpets and lightening, and the people are afraid.

When he comes again, it is in a very different way. Can you think of what it is?

I'll give you a hint. It involves a girl, and a stable, and the only people who know about it at first are some shepherds.

Prayer: God who keeps promises, who reveals yourself in cloud and fire and thunder, thank you that you are merciful. Thank you that you speak, and that you are gentle when we are afraid. Help us to remember that you have always wanted to be with us, and speak to us.

DECEMBER 10

How God Treats the Poor

5 'Now then, if you will indeed obey My voice and keep My covenant, then you shall be My own possession among all the peoples, for all the earth is Mine; 6 and **you shall be to Me a kingdom of priests and a holy nation.**' (Exodus 19:5-6)

22 'When you reap the harvest of your land, moreover, you shall not reap to the very corners of your field nor gather the gleaning of your harvest ; **you are to leave them for the needy and the alien.** I am the LORD your God.' " (Leviticus 23:22 NASB)

12 "Now, Israel, what does the LORD your God require from you, but to fear the LORD your God, to walk in all His ways and love Him, and to serve the LORD your God with all your heart and with all your soul, 13 and to keep the LORD'S commandments and His statutes which I am commanding you today for your good ? 14 "Behold, to the LORD your God belong heaven and the highest heavens, the earth and all that is in it. 15 "Yet on your fathers did the LORD set His affection to love them, and He chose their descendants after them, even you above all peoples, as it is this day. 16 "So circumcise your heart, and stiffen your neck no longer. 17 "For the LORD your God is the God of gods and the Lord of lords, the great, the mighty, and the awesome God who does not show partiality nor take a bribe. 18 **"He executes justice for the orphan and the widow, and shows His love for the alien by giving him food and**

clothing. 19 "So show your love for the alien, for you were aliens in the land of Egypt. 20 "You shall fear the LORD your God ; you shall serve Him and cling to Him, and you shall swear by His name. 21 "He is your praise and He is your God, who has done these great and awesome things for you which your eyes have seen. 22 "Your fathers went down to Egypt seventy persons in all, and now the LORD your God has made you as numerous as the stars of heaven. (Deuteronomy 10:12-21 NASB)

"At the end of every third year you shall bring out all the tithe of your produce in that year, and shall deposit it in your town. 29 "The Levite, because he has no portion or inheritance among you, and the **alien, the orphan and the widow who are in your town, shall come and eat and be satisfied,** in order that the LORD your God may bless you in all the work of your hand which you do. (Deuteronomy 14:28-29 NASB)

15 "You shall not hand over to his master a slave who has escaped from his master to you. 16 "He shall live with you in your midst, in the place which he shall choose in one of your towns where it pleases him; you shall not mistreat him. (Deuteronomy 23:15-16 NASB)

10 "When you make your neighbor a loan of any sort, you shall not enter his house to take his pledge. 11 "You shall remain outside, and the man to whom you make the loan shall bring the pledge out to you. 12 "If he is a poor man, you shall not sleep with his pledge. 13 "When the sun goes down you shall surely return the pledge to him, that he may sleep in his cloak and bless you; and it will be righteousness for you before the LORD your God. 14 **"You shall not oppress a hired servant who is poor and needy,** whether he is one of your countrymen or one of your aliens who is in your land in your towns. 15 "You shall give him his wages on his day before the sun sets, for he is poor and sets his heart on it; so that he will not cry against you to the LORD and it become

sin in you. 16 "Fathers shall not be put to death for their sons, nor shall sons be put to death for their fathers ; everyone shall be put to death for his own sin. 17 **"You shall not pervert the justice due an alien or an orphan, nor take a widow's garment in pledge.** 18 "But you shall remember that you were a slave in Egypt, and that the LORD your God redeemed you from there ; therefore I am commanding you to do this thing. 19 "When you reap your harvest in your field and have forgotten a sheaf in the field, you shall not go back to get it; it shall be for the alien, for the orphan, and for the widow, in order that the LORD your God may bless you in all the work of your hands. 20 "When you beat your olive tree, you shall not go over the boughs again ; it shall be for the alien, for the orphan, and for the widow. 21 "When you gather the grapes of your vineyard, you shall not go over it again ; it shall be for the alien, for the orphan, and for the widow. 22 "You shall remember that you were a slave in the land of Egypt ; therefore I am commanding you to do this thing. (Deuteronomy 24:10-22 NASB)

Yesterday we talked about how God met the people of Israel on Mount Sinai. There he told Moses his plans for Israel, what it was that he wanted. He said that he would make them a kingdom of priests, and a holy nation.

What do you think that means?

Do you know what it is that priests do?

Priests are the people that go between everyone else, and the God they worship. In the time of Moses people worshiped all sorts of gods in many different kinds of temples. Most of these gods were represented by statues made of metal or wood and the priests would tell the people what the gods wanted from them, and help the people to ask for favors from the gods.

What God wanted for Israel is that all of them would know him, would know how to tell people what he was like and what he wanted, and be able to go to God on the behalf of others. If the whole nation was full of priests, and holy to God, who would they show God to if everyone in Israel already knew Him? Any guesses?

If you guessed the rest of the world, you got it right. God wants Israel to display what He is like to the rest of the world.

As Moses talks to God on the mountain God starts to tell him about how he wants the Israelites to behave, in order to be the kind of people that show the world what God is like.

God cares about justice, about the poor, and the needy, and the oppressed, the woman who is all alone, the children who have no food, the stranger in a strange land. God cares about how those people are treated. He tells the Israelites to make sure they have food, that they are treated fairly, that they are helped. Because that's what God is like, he cares about the people in need.

Prayer: God of justice and mercy, thank you that you made us to know you, and show others what you are like. Help us to be your presence here on the earth. Help us to care for the poor, needy, and oppressed as you do. May people see your character and your love through our actions.

DECEMBER 11

God's Jubilee

10 'You shall thus consecrate the fiftieth year and proclaim a release through the land to all its inhabitants. **It shall be a jubilee for you, and each of you shall return to his own property, and each of you shall return to his family.** 11 'You shall have the fiftieth year as a jubilee ; you shall not sow, nor reap its aftergrowth, nor gather in from its untrimmed vines. 12 'For it is a jubilee ; it shall be holy to you. You shall eat its crops out of the field. 13 'On this year of jubilee each of you shall return to his own property. 14 'If you make a sale, moreover, to your friend or buy from your friend's hand, you shall not wrong one another. 15 'Corresponding to the number of years after the jubilee, you shall buy from your friend ; he is to sell to you according to the number of years of crops. 16 'In proportion to the extent of the years you shall increase its price, and in proportion to the fewness of the years you shall diminish its price, for it is a number of crops he is selling to you. 17 'So you shall not wrong one another, but you shall fear your God ; for I am the LORD your God. 18 'You shall thus observe My statutes and keep My judgments, so as to carry them out, that you may live securely on the land. 19 'Then the land will yield its produce, so that you can eat your fill and live securely on it. 20 'But if you say, "What are we going to eat on the seventh year if we do not sow or gather in our crops ?" 21 then I will so order My blessing for

you in the sixth year that it will bring forth the crop for three years. 22 'When you are sowing the eighth year, you can still eat old things from the crop, eating the old until the ninth year when its crop comes in.

23 'The land, moreover, shall not be sold permanently, for the land is Mine; for you are but aliens and sojourners with Me. 24 'Thus for every piece of your property, you are to provide for the redemption of the land. 25 'If a fellow countryman of yours becomes so poor he has to sell part of his property, then his nearest kinsman is to come and buy back what his relative has sold. 26 'Or in case a man has no kinsman, but so recovers his means as to find sufficient for its redemption, 27 then he shall calculate the years since its sale and refund the balance to the man to whom he sold it, and so return to his property. 28 **'But if he has not found sufficient means to get it back for himself, then what he has sold shall remain in the hands of its purchaser until the year of jubilee ; but at the jubilee it shall revert, that he may return to his property.** (Leviticus 25:10-28 NASB)

35 'Now in case a countryman of yours becomes poor and his means with regard to you falter, then **you are to sustain him, like a stranger or a sojourner, that he may live with you.** 36 'Do not take usurious interest from him, but revere your God, that your countryman may live with you. 37 'You shall not give him your silver at interest, nor your food for gain. 38 'I am the LORD your God, who brought you out of the land of Egypt to give you the land of Canaan and to be your God. 39 **'If a countryman of yours becomes so poor with regard to you that he sells himself to you, you shall not subject him to a slave's service. 40 'He shall be with you as a hired man, as if he were a sojourner ; he shall serve with you until the year of jubilee. 41 'He shall then go out from you, he and his sons with him, and shall go back to his family, that he may return to the property of his forefathers. 42** 'For they are My

servants whom I brought out from the land of Egypt ;
they are not to be sold in a slave sale. 43 'You shall
not rule over him with severity, but are to revere
your God. (Leviticus 25:35-43 NASB)

Did any of what we just read make sense to you? It might have seemed
kind of boring. But once you understand what it's saying it's really,
really amazing.

One of the things that happens a lot in this world is that some
people have enough money or resources at the right time to own a lot
of stuff: land, or factories, or other things that have a lot of value
because people need them to survive. What happens is that those
people who own everything can hire other people to work for them
and they get richer, and richer, while other people end up with less,
and less. All over the world today you can see examples of poor
people living on land they don't own, paying much of what they make
to the person who owns the land they are farming, or the tools they
need to work to make a living, or the place they need to go and work
in. They have to pay such a big portion of what they earn to the person
who owns everything that they barely have enough for their family to
eat and survive.

The person who owns everything gets richer from other people's
hard work, and those people get poorer because it is so hard for them
to survive. They can't plan ahead or save anything for emergencies. So
when someone gets sick or they need money they have to borrow it
from someone else, and then sometimes that person makes them or
one of their children work for them for free until they can pay back the
money.

God told Israel to do things differently. He said that once every 50
years everything went back to the original owners. People who were
working for someone else to pay off a debt got to go back to their
families. And if you owed anyone a lot of money and couldn't pay it
back your debt was cancelled.

That's amazing!

Have you ever sold or lost something that was important to you?

Would you like it if there was a way you could get it back and start over?

Doing it God's way makes it so that no one can really get to the point where they own everything and everyone works for them. The people who were having hard times, they get to start over again. They get everything back and they get a second chance.

Imagine if that were to happen today in your country. I bet you know at least one person, you may not know this about them, who owes a lot of money to someone else. A lot of people in the US have been having very hard times because they owed someone money and couldn't pay because times got hard. Lots of people have lost their houses, their jobs.

God wanted Israel to be a different sort of place. A place where they took care of each other and didn't get rich off of someone's hardship.

If someone runs out of money, they were to take care of them, to help them, to let them live with them and help them through hard times. God reminded them over and over that they all belonged to Him.

If someone is God's person, you should probably take care of them. And if the land you are using is God's land, and he's just letting you use it, then you should probably take care of it like he tells you to.

He tells them to even let the land rest. Every farmer today knows that you need to let soil rest every so often in order for it to be able to keep producing crops. The Israelites didn't know that. But if they obeyed God about letting the land rest they would have good soil for good crops anyway.

This was another way that Israel would be different from all the nations around it. It would be one more way that they shone the light of God's love and justice to the people who were paying attention. This is part of God's plan to bless all of the world.

Prayer: God who returns slaves to their families, lands to those whose families have lost everything, help us to live in the same spirit of generosity.

Help us to live in cooperation with your creation, to trust your wisdom, to give times of rest to people, and to land. Help us to shine the light of your love and justice on the world. Help our life here to be a blessing to all.

DECEMBER 12

How Rahab Becomes Part of God's Story

4 But the woman had taken the two men and hidden them, and she said, "Yes, the men came to me, but I did not know where they were from. 5 "It came about when it was time to shut the gate at dark, that the men went out; I do not know where the men went. Pursue them quickly, for you will overtake them." 6 But she had brought them up to the roof and hidden them in the stalks of flax which she had laid in order on the roof. 7 So the men pursued them on the road to the Jordan to the fords ; and as soon as those who were pursuing them had gone out, they shut the gate. 8 Now before they lay down, she came up to them on the roof, 9 and said to the men, "I know that the LORD has given you the land, and that the terror of you has fallen on us, and that all the inhabitants of the land have melted away before you. 10 "For we have heard how the LORD dried up the water of the Red Sea before you when you came out of Egypt, and what you did to the two kings of the Amorites who were beyond the Jordan, to Sihon and Og, whom you utterly destroyed. 11 "When we heard it, our hearts melted and no courage remained in any man any longer because of you; for the LORD your God, He is God in heaven above and on earth beneath . 12 "Now therefore, please swear to me by the LORD, since I have dealt kindly with you, that you also will deal kindly with my father's household, and give me a pledge of truth, 13 and spare my father and my

mother and my brothers and my sisters, with all who belong to them, and deliver our lives from death." 14 So the men said to her, "Our life for yours if you do not tell this business of ours; and it shall come about when the LORD gives us the land that we will deal kindly and faithfully with you." (Joshua 2:4 -14)

Rahab was not what the Israelites would have called a respectable woman. She was also one of the enemy, the people who were in the land that God had promised to Abraham, Isaac and Jacob so many, many years ago. But, God wasn't just giving the land to the Israelites. He was on their side and helping them, but he wanted them to fight for the land, to make them strong.

Rahab, even though she was the enemy, helped the two men that Joshua, the new leader of the Israelites, sent to spy out the land. Joshua wanted to know what they were up against. She told them how everyone was afraid of them, because they had heard how God fought for them, and did many wonders, and how they had defeated everyone who got in their way. She was sure they were going to win the coming fight, and she wanted to be on their side.

She chose to protect them and asked them to help her in return. The men promised that they would help her, and they did.

Rahab joined Israel. She married an Israelite and God chose her and the children who came through her to be part of the line of people through whom His promised blessing would come. Just like Abraham, and Sarah, and Isaac, and Rebekah, the children of Rahab, who wasn't good enough in the eyes of a lot of people, would be how He brought this promise to the world.

Rahab chose God's side, and He blessed her for it.

Sometimes it's not as clear which side God is on, or what we should do. Do you ever wonder what they right thing to do in a situation is? How do you figure it out?

Prayer: God who accepts all who turn to you, accept us as we are, as we turn to you. Help us to know when we are opposing you, and turn toward you instead. Give us the wisdom to know what to do to help your plans succeed. Thank you that no one is excluded from your story, your plans. You include all kinds of people in your plan for redemption.

DECEMBER 13

Righteousness is Hard Without the BREATH OF LIFE

6 When Joshua had dismissed the people, the sons of Israel went each to his inheritance to possess the land. 7 The people served the LORD all the days of Joshua, and all the days of the elders who survived Joshua, who had seen all the great work of the LORD which He had done for Israel. 8 Then Joshua the son of Nun, the servant of the LORD, died at the age of one hundred and ten. 9 And they buried him in the territory of his inheritance in Timnath-heres, in the hill country of Ephraim, north of Mount Gaash. 10 All that generation also were gathered to their fathers ; and there arose another generation after them who did not know the LORD, nor yet the work which He had done for Israel. 11 Then the sons of Israel did evil in the sight of the LORD and served the Baals, 12 and they forsook the LORD, the God of their fathers, who had brought them out of the land of Egypt, and followed other gods from among the gods of the peoples who were around them, and bowed themselves down to them; thus they provoked the LORD to anger. 13 So they forsook the LORD and served Baal and the Ashtaroth. 14 The anger of the LORD burned against Israel, and He gave them into the hands of plunderers who plundered them; and He sold them into the hands of their enemies around them, so that they could no longer stand before their enemies. 15 Wherever they went, the hand of the LORD was against them for evil, as the LORD had

spoken and as the LORD had sworn to them, so that they were severely distressed. 16 Then the LORD raised up judges who delivered them from the hands of those who plundered them. 17 Yet they did not listen to their judges, for they played the harlot after other gods and bowed themselves down to them. They turned aside quickly from the way in which their fathers had walked in obeying the commandments of the LORD ; they did not do as their fathers. 18 When the LORD raised up judges for them, the LORD was with the judge and delivered them from the hand of their enemies all the days of the judge ; for the LORD was moved to pity by their groaning because of those who oppressed and afflicted them. 19 But it came about when the judge died, that they would turn back and act more corruptly than their fathers, in following other gods to serve them and bow down to them; they did not abandon their practices or their stubborn ways. 20 So the anger of the LORD burned against Israel, and He said, "Because this nation has transgressed My covenant which I commanded their fathers and has not listened to My voice, 21 I also will no longer drive out before them any of the nations which Joshua left when he died, 22 in order to test Israel by them, whether they will keep the way of the LORD to walk in it as their fathers did, or not." (Judges 2:6-22 NASB)

As God promised, the people of Israel do finally live in the land of Canaan. For as long as those who walked with God in the wilderness lived, the people remembered God, and remembered to do all that He had commanded them. But then those people died. Their children and grandchildren did not know God as they had done, and they did not obey God's commands.

There had been a complication. There were still other people living in the land of Canaan. The Israelites had conquered the land, but there were other people who had been living in Canaan first. Many of them still lived in the land. Those people worshiped different gods and had different customs. To the children of the Israelites those gods seemed pretty interesting. They worshiped the Baals and forgot the ways of God.

God allowed them to be oppressed and defeated by the people groups around them. When they stopped obeying God, he stopped protecting them. It's funny how when times were easy they forgot how God had helped them in the past, but when it got hard, they remembered God and turned to him.

So God stopped protecting Israel, and it got very hard. Then God raised up a judge. There were men and women who God raised up and called to free his people and bring them back to God again. As long as those people lived Israel remembered to worship and obey God. But when they died Israel went right back to doing whatever they wanted and suffered for it; over, and over, and over, and over again.

Have you ever done something you weren't supposed to and then suffered and felt bad about it when something unpleasant happened to you as a consequence? Did you ever do that thing a separate time, after forgetting how much you didn't enjoy the consequences the first time around? I knew a boy who would never bring a sweater with him on a chilly day. His mother reminded him to bring a sweater, but he decided not to and got very cold. But once he got home and got warm he forgot all about it. The next time his mom said to bring a sweater he still didn't bring one. No matter how many times he felt cold, and his mom reminded him, he still couldn't seem to remember to bring a sweater.

Israel just wouldn't learn from their mistakes. They seemed to do a pretty bad job of teaching their children to learn from their mistakes too, because the next generation was always making the same mistakes their parents had.

Do you remember when we talked about how Adam and Eve, and all of us, lost the Breath of Life in the garden when they disobeyed God? Without the Breath of Life, without God's spirit in us, obeying him was so incredibly hard. We just didn't have the power to live as we were made to live it without God constantly beside us, reminding us of what to do.

* * *

This was a problem. It wasn't just a problem for Israel, it was a problem for everyone. We just didn't have the power to be good, to do the good things God told us on his own. We needed help. **The Israelites still needed the Breath of Life back in them.** But it's going to be a while before that happens. They are going to learn some pretty hard lessons along the way.

Prayer: God of Life, who gave us breath. Thank you that you know how hard it is for us to obey you. Thank you that you breath your life into us, and you didn't leave us alone to try and obey on our own power. You had a plan to give us the help we needed. You taught your people again and again to return to you, that you were the source of their life and abundance. Help us to ask you for help when we are suffering, even if it's our own fault that we are in the mess that we're in. Help us to remember you even when things are easy, and life is good. Help us to breath your breath and your life into our lungs.

DECEMBER 14

Ruth and Boaz Remember God

1 Now it came about in the days when the judges governed, that there was a famine in the land. And a certain man of Bethlehem in Judah went to sojourn in the land of Moab with his wife and his two sons. 2 The name of the man was Elimelech, and the name of his wife, Naomi ; and the names of his two sons were Mahlon and Chilion, Ephrathites of Bethlehem in Judah. Now they entered the land of Moab and remained there. 3 Then Elimelech, Naomi's husband, died ; and she was left with her two sons. 4 They took for themselves Moabite women as wives ; the name of the one was Orpah and the name of the other Ruth. And they lived there about ten years. 5 Then both Mahlon and Chilion also died, and the woman was bereft of her two children and her husband. 6 Then she arose with her daughters-in-law that she might return from the land of Moab, for she had heard in the land of Moab that the LORD had visited His people in giving them food. 7 So she departed from the place where she was, and her two daughters-in-law with her; and they went on the way to return to the land of Judah. 8 And Naomi said to her two daughters-in-law, "Go, return each of you to her mother's house. May the LORD deal kindly with you as you have dealt with the dead and with me. 9 "May the LORD grant that you may find rest, each in the house of her husband." Then she kissed them, and they lifted up their voices and wept. 10 And they said

to her, "No, but we will surely return with you to your people." 11 But Naomi said, "Return, my daughters. Why should you go with me? Have I yet sons in my womb, that they may be your husbands ? 12 "Return, my daughters ! Go, for I am too old to have a husband. If I said I have hope, if I should even have a husband tonight and also bear sons, 13 would you therefore wait until they were grown ? Would you therefore refrain from marrying ? No, my daughters ; for it is harder for me than for you, for the hand of the LORD has gone forth against me."

14 And they lifted up their voices and wept again ; and Orpah kissed her mother-in-law, but Ruth clung to her. 15 Then she said, "Behold, your sister-in-law has gone back to her people and her gods ; return after your sister-in-law." 16 But Ruth said, "Do not urge me to leave you or turn back from following you; for where you go, I will go, and where you lodge, I will lodge. Your people shall be my people, and your God, my God. 17 "Where you die, I will die, and there I will be buried. Thus may the LORD do to me, and worse , if anything but death parts you and me." 18 When she saw that she was determined to go with her, she said no more to her. 19 So they both went until they came to Bethlehem. (Ruth 1:1-19 NASB)

1 Now Naomi had a kinsman of her husband, a man of great wealth, of the family of Elimelech, whose name was Boaz. 2 And Ruth the Moabitess said to Naomi, "Please let me go to the field and glean among the ears of grain after one in whose sight I may find favor." And she said to her, "Go, my daughter." 3 So she departed and went and gleaned in the field after the reapers ; and she happened to come to the portion of the field belonging to Boaz, who was of the family of Elimelech. 4 Now behold, Boaz came from Bethlehem and said to the reapers, "May the LORD be with you." And they said to him, "May the LORD bless you." 5 Then Boaz said to his servant who was in charge of the reapers, "Whose

young woman is this ?" 6 The servant in charge of the reapers replied, "She is the young Moabite woman who returned with Naomi from the land of Moab. 7 "And she said, 'Please let me glean and gather after the reapers among the sheaves.' Thus she came and has remained from the morning until now ; she has been sitting in the house for a little while." 8 Then Boaz said to Ruth, "Listen carefully, my daughter. Do not go to glean in another field ; furthermore, do not go on from this one, but stay here with my maids. 9 "Let your eyes be on the field which they reap, and go after them. Indeed, I have commanded the servants not to touch you. When you are thirsty, go to the water jars and drink from what the servants draw." 10 Then she fell on her face, bowing to the ground and said to him, "Why have I found favor in your sight that you should take notice of me, since I am a foreigner ?" 11 Boaz replied to her, "All that you have done for your mother-in-law after the death of your husband has been fully reported to me, and how you left your father and your mother and the land of your birth, and came to a people that you did not previously know. 12 "May the LORD reward your work, and your wages be full from the LORD, the God of Israel, under whose wings you have come to seek refuge." (Ruth 2:1-12)

You may have heard this story before. Can you tell me how it ends for Ruth?

Boaz marries her, and God give her a son, and Naomi is happy, and that son turns out to be the great, great grandfather of a king! Guess who Boaz's great great grandmother was? (Hint: She used to live in Jericho. Her name was Rahab.) Boaz and Ruth are the continuation of her story, just as they are the continuation of Abraham, Isaac and Jacob's story of promise.

This story takes place in the time of the judges, when much of Israel was forgetting to obey God and doing wicked, wicked things to each other. But here we have Ruth, who isn't even from Israel, choosing to stay with her old mother in law and take care of her because she has no one left who will. Ruth chooses this freely. She doesn't have to stay with Naomi. We also have Boaz, who has remembered God's law, and allows the poor in the community to go after his laborers and pick up the grain that they miss. Do you remember when we talked about how God commanded them to take care of the poor like that?

So Boaz is keeping God's law, and Ruth is caring for her old mother in law who is poor and has nothing left. These two people see each other and care about each other right away. Boaz likes Ruth, not just because she's probably pretty, but because she has the kind of character and heart that care about others. Ruth likes Boaz because he is kind to her, and protects her and takes care of her and Naomi. It works out very well then that the law puts Boaz in a position where he can marry Ruth, and redeem what was lost to Naomi by raising up a family in honor of her lost husband and sons.

The children of these two people will remember to follow God. These two people will have grandsons and great grandsons who obey God and know him as they do.

God blesses them, because they remember Him. The promised blessing will come through them as well.

Prayer: God who redeems and restores what has been lost, our kinsman redeemer, thank you that you meet us where we are, in our time of need, our time of distress, and you provide more than we can imagine. Help us to have the courage to choose you, and to be faithful to your commands, even when we have lost everything. Remind us that you are always at work to bring beauty and joy where once there was only ashes and mourning.

DECEMBER 15

God's Prophet

1 Now the boy Samuel was ministering to the LORD before Eli. And word from the LORD was rare in those days, visions were infrequent . 2 It happened at that time as Eli was lying down in his place (now his eyesight had begun to grow dim and he could not see well), 3 and the lamp of God had not yet gone out, and Samuel was lying down in the temple of the LORD where the ark of God was, 4 that the LORD called Samuel ; and he said, "Here I am." 5 Then he ran to Eli and said, "Here I am, for you called me." But he said, "I did not call, lie down again." So he went and lay down. 6 The LORD called yet again, "Samuel !" So Samuel arose and went to Eli and said, "Here I am, for you called me." But he answered, "I did not call, my son, lie down again." 7 Now Samuel did not yet know the LORD, nor had the word of the LORD yet been revealed to him. 8 So the LORD called Samuel again for the third time. And he arose and went to Eli and said, "Here I am, for you called me." Then Eli discerned that the LORD was calling the boy. 9 And Eli said to Samuel, "Go lie down, and it shall be if He calls you, that you shall say, 'Speak, LORD, for Your servant is listening.' " So Samuel went and lay down in his place. 10 Then the LORD came and stood and called as at other times, "Samuel ! Samuel !" And Samuel said, "Speak, for Your servant is listening." 11 The LORD said to Samuel, "Behold, I am about to do a thing in Israel at

which both ears of everyone who hears it will tingle.

19 Thus Samuel grew and the LORD was with him and let none of his words fail . 20 All Israel from Dan even to Beersheba knew that Samuel was confirmed as a prophet of the LORD. 21 And the LORD appeared again at Shiloh, because the LORD revealed Himself to Samuel at Shiloh by the word of the LORD." (1 Samuel 3:1-21)

"The word of the LORD was rare in those days, visions were infrequent."

Think about all the interesting things that sentence tells us. Can you think of them?

God talked to people, sometimes more often than others. At this time in Israel, not very many people heard from God. But the Bible tells us that this wasn't always the case. In other times people heard from God more often.

People had visions. God talked to His people through visions. At least, some people, and they told the others what they saw and heard.

But right now, not many people heard from God, until Samuel. Samuel was a prophet. God chose him to speak to the people for him. Remember when Moses spoke to the people for God? God was still finding ways to speak to the people. He called Judges to free the people, and he called prophets to speak to the people for him.

Samuel was also a child given to a woman who couldn't have children, after she prayed to God. God seems to like to do that doesn't He? He likes to give women who ask him the children they haven't been able to have. In Samuel's case, his mother was so grateful that she dedicated him to God's service and God called him as a prophet when he was very small. He was a very important part of Israel's story at this point. The blessing that is to come through Israel has much to do with what Samuel hears from God and how he obeys.

More on that tomorrow.

* * *

Prayer: God who speaks, thank you that you give us your words, thank you that you are alive and speak to your people. Help us, your people, to know your voice and to recognize you in all the ways that you speak to us . Help us to also reply, "Speak Lord, for your servant is listening."

DECEMBER 16

Give Us a King!

1 And it came about when Samuel was old that he appointed his sons judges over Israel. 2 Now the name of his firstborn was Joel, and the name of his second, Abijah ; they were judging in Beersheba. 3 His sons, however, did not walk in his ways, but turned aside after dishonest gain and took bribes and perverted justice. 4 Then all the elders of Israel gathered together and came to Samuel at Ramah ; 5 and they said to him, "Behold, you have grown old, and your sons do not walk in your ways. **Now appoint a king for us to judge us like all the nations."** 6 But the thing was displeasing in the sight of Samuel when they said, "Give us a king to judge us." And Samuel prayed to the LORD. 7 The LORD said to Samuel, "Listen to the voice of the people in regard to all that they say to you, for they have not rejected you, but **they have rejected Me from being king over them.** 8 "Like all the deeds which they have done since the day that I brought them up from Egypt even to this day -in that they have forsaken Me and served other gods -so they are doing to you also. 9 "Now then, listen to their voice ; however, you shall solemnly warn them and tell them of the procedure of the king who will reign over them."

10 So Samuel spoke all the words of the LORD to the people who had asked of him a king. 11 He said, "This will be the procedure of the king who will reign over you: **he will take your sons** and place them for

himself in his chariots and among his horsemen and they will run before his chariots. 12 "He will appoint for himself commanders of thousands and of fifties, and some to do his plowing and to reap his harvest and to make his weapons of war and equipment for his chariots. 13 "**He will also take your daughters** for perfumers and cooks and bakers. 14 "**He will take the best of your fields and your vineyards and your olive groves** and give them to his servants. 15 "He will take a tenth of your seed and of your vineyards and give to his officers and to his servants. 16 "He will also take your male servants and your female servants and your best young men and your donkeys and use them for his work. 17 "He will take a tenth of your flocks, and **you yourselves will become his servants.** 18 "Then you will cry out in that day because of your king whom you have chosen for yourselves, but the LORD will not answer you in that day." 19 Nevertheless, the people refused to listen to the voice of Samuel, and they said, **"No, but there shall be a king over us, 20 that we also may be like all the nations, that our king may judge us and go out before us and fight our battles."** 21 Now after Samuel had heard all the words of the people, he repeated them in the LORD'S hearing. 22 The LORD said to Samuel, "Listen to their voice and appoint them a king." So Samuel said to the men of Israel, "Go every man to his city." (1 Samuel 8:1-22 NASB)

The people of Israel want to be like all the other nations around them. Instead of waiting for God to raise up a just judge, such as Samuel, they want a king. They want someone to be their judge and fight their battles and they want to be like all of the nations around them.

Do you think God wants for them to be like everyone else around them?

Wasn't God supposed to be their king?

Why do you think that God tells Samuel to give them what they want?

There are lots of times in the Bible when God gives people things when they insist on having them, even when he knows it's not the best choice. Sometimes the only way to learn that what you want isn't the best thing for you to have is to experience it for yourself. Israel will get what they want, and then they will be forced to serve these kings they have asked for. It will go badly for them. Especially when those kings don't act righteously, which, most of them won't.

Giving Israel a human king to rule over them is not God's first plan.

The last several hundred years of our history here on earth has consisted of people finally getting rid of kings that ruled over them whom they were forced to serve. It has consisted of more nations having governments that give them a say in what happens to them, and where the people are in charge of themselves. Israel had that in the beginning, but they didn't want it. They gave it away so they could be like all the other nations around them and not have to think for themselves about what was right and wrong.

But God can work with this change of plan, even if it's not what he wanted. For through these human kings, he will lead them, after a long, long time, to the true king. God will be their king once more.

Prayer: Thank you God that you can work through whatever we bring to you. Thank you that when we reject plan A, you have a Plan B, and a Plan C, and that in spite of our stubbornness and the ways we reject your best plans for us, you still are able to bring about your will, and accomplish your redemption, just as you did for Israel. Help us to trust in your plans. Help us to trust that you can redeem our poor choices. Thank you that you never abandon us.

DECEMBER 17

A King With God's Heart

1 Now the LORD said to Samuel, "How long will you
grieve over Saul, since I have rejected him from being
king over Israel ? Fill your horn with oil and go ; I
will send you to Jesse the Bethlehemite, for I have
selected a king for Myself among his sons." 2 But
Samuel said, "How can I go ? When Saul hears of it,
he will kill me." And the LORD said, "Take a heifer
with you and say, 'I have come to sacrifice to the
LORD.' 3 "You shall invite Jesse to the sacrifice, and I
will show you what you shall do ; and you shall
anoint for Me the one whom I designate to you." 4 So
Samuel did what the LORD said, and came to
Bethlehem. And the elders of the city came trembling
to meet him and said, "Do you come in peace ?" 5 He
said, "In peace ; I have come to sacrifice to the LORD.
Consecrate yourselves and come with me to the
sacrifice." He also consecrated Jesse and his sons and
invited them to the sacrifice. 6 When they entered, he
looked at Eliab and thought, "Surely the LORD'S
anointed is before Him." 7 But the LORD said to
Samuel, "Do not look at his appearance or at the
height of his stature, because I have rejected him; for
God sees not as man sees, for man looks at the
outward appearance, but the LORD looks at the
heart." 8 Then Jesse called Abinadab and made him
pass before Samuel. And he said, "The LORD has not
chosen this one either." 9 Next Jesse made Shammah
pass by. And he said, "The LORD has not chosen this

one either." 10 Thus Jesse made seven of his sons pass before Samuel. But Samuel said to Jesse, "The LORD has not chosen these." 11 And Samuel said to Jesse, "Are these all the children ?" And he said, "There remains yet the youngest, and behold, he is tending the sheep." Then Samuel said to Jesse, "Send and bring him; for we will not sit down until he comes here." David Anointed 12 So he sent and brought him in. Now he was ruddy, with beautiful eyes and a handsome appearance. And the LORD said, "Arise, anoint him; for this is he." 13 Then Samuel took the horn of oil and anointed him in the midst of his brothers ; and the Spirit of the LORD came mightily upon David from that day forward. And Samuel arose and went to Ramah. (1 Samuel 16:1-13 NASB)

When God gave Israel a king, he first chose Saul. But Saul became proud and overstepped his position and God was displeased with him. So God chose himself a new king, and he sent Samuel to anoint him. It would take years before David would actually become the king of Israel. He would have to wait for Saul to die, and Saul would make his life miserable for a long time before then.

But God chose David, and God's spirit was very strong with him, and David was a mostly good man. He acted as God would want him to act.

There was this one time, he did something very wrong, and he and all the people suffered as a result. But even then, he turned to God, and God forgave him.

David was, in a lot of ways, the kind of king God wanted for Israel to have, even though he was human, and still made mistakes. His heart was the kind of heart God looks for.

It is the descendants of David that God establishes on the throne of of Israel. It is descendants of David who are considered by Israel to be the true kings. It will be a descendant of David who will bring deliverance.

* * *

1 Then a shoot will spring from the stem of Jesse, And a branch from his roots will bear fruit. 2 The Spirit of the LORD will rest on Him, The spirit of wisdom and understanding, The spirit of counsel and strength, The spirit of knowledge and the fear of the LORD. 3 And He will delight in the fear of the LORD, And He will not judge by what His eyes see, Nor make a decision by what His ears hear ; 4 But with righteousness He will judge the poor, And decide with fairness for the afflicted of the earth ... 9 They will not hurt or destroy in all My holy mountain, For the earth will be full of the knowledge of the LORD As the waters cover the sea. (Isaiah 11:1-4, 9 NASB)

Who was Jesse again? That's right, David's father.

In a dark, dark time, when all in Israel think hope is lost, God sends this promise, that there will be a king again, a righteous king with God's spirit in him. This is the hope they cling to when it seems all is lost. This is the hope we all cling to when it seems that all is lost, that God will still keep his promise that he made, so long ago.

Prayer: God of kings, promise keeper, thank you for the hope that you give. Thank you that you promised that a time would come when all that is wrong will be made right. Help us to turn to you in all things. Help us to have hearts like yours, filled with compassion for those who are poor and afflicted. Thank you that you judge things differently, and more wisely, than we humans judge. Thank you that you look at our hearts.

DECEMBER 18

The Kings, and the People, Reject God

2 Jehoahaz was twenty-three years old when he became king, and he reigned in Jerusalem three months. 3 The king of Egypt dethroned him in Jerusalem and imposed on Judah a levy of a hundred talents of silver and a talent of gold. 4 The king of Egypt made Eliakim, a brother of Jehoahaz, king over Judah and Jerusalem and changed Eliakim's name to Jehoiakim. But Neco took Eliakim's brother Jehoahaz and carried him off to Egypt.

5 Jehoiakim was twenty-five years old when he became king, and he reigned in Jerusalem eleven years. **He did evil in the eyes of the LORD his God.** 6 Nebuchadnezzar king of Babylon attacked him and bound him with bronze shackles to take him to Babylon. 7 Nebuchadnezzar also took to Babylon articles from the temple of the LORD and put them in his temple there. 8 The other events of Jehoiakim's reign, the detestable things he did and all that was found against him, are written in the book of the kings of Israel and Judah. And Jehoiachin his son succeeded him as king.

9 Jehoiachin was eighteen years old when he became king, and he reigned in Jerusalem three months and ten days. **He did evil in the eyes of the LORD.** 10 In the spring, King Nebuchadnezzar sent for him and brought him to Babylon, together with articles of value from the temple of the LORD, and he made Jehoiachin's uncle, Zedekiah, king over Judah

and Jerusalem.

11 Zedekiah was twenty-one years old when he became king, and he reigned in Jerusalem eleven years. 12 **He did evil in the eyes of the LORD his God and did not humble himself before Jeremiah the prophet, who spoke the word of the LORD.** 13 He also rebelled against King Nebuchadnezzar, who had made him take an oath in God's name. **He became stiff-necked and hardened his heart and would not turn to the LORD, the God of Israel. 14 Furthermore, all the leaders of the priests and the people became more and more unfaithful, following all the detestable practices of the nations and defiling the temple of the LORD, which he had consecrated in Jerusalem.**

15 **The LORD, the God of their fathers, sent word to them through his messengers again and again, because he had pity on his people and on his dwelling place.** 16 But they mocked God's messengers, despised his words and scoffed at his prophets until the wrath of the LORD was aroused against his people and there was no remedy. 17 He brought up against them the king of the Babylonians, who killed their young men with the sword in the sanctuary, and spared neither young man nor young woman, old man or aged. God handed all of them over to Nebuchadnezzar. 18 He carried to Babylon all the articles from the temple of God, both large and small, and the treasures of the LORD's temple and the treasures of the king and his officials. 19 They set fire to God's temple and broke down the wall of Jerusalem; they burned all the palaces and destroyed everything of value there. 20 He carried into exile to Babylon the remnant, who escaped from the sword, and they became servants to him and his sons until the kingdom of Persia came to power. 21 **The land enjoyed its sabbath rests; all the time of its desolation it rested, until the seventy years were completed** in fulfillment of the word of the LORD spoken by Jeremiah. (2 Chronicles 361-21 NASB)

* * *

It's been hundreds of years since David became king of Israel. Not very long after, most of the tribes of Israel rejected David's grandson as king and set up their own king. The land of Israel was split into two kingdoms, north and south. The northern kingdom abandoned God so quickly that by the time of what we just read, they had all been carried off into captivity by other countries and were no longer a country. Only Judah remained.

But Judah's kings, and priests, and people had become increasingly evil, and proud, and foolish. They angered foreign kings, they angered God by worshiping other gods. God sent prophet after prophet to warn them of what would happen if they didn't change their ways and obey God again, but they wouldn't listen.

So God stopped protecting them.

All of them were carried off, out of the promised land, into exile in Babylon. They served the king of Babylon now, and its people. The kingdoms of Judah and Israel were no more. They had completely failed to be the people who showed God to the world. **They had become exactly like the rest of the world instead.**

It seems like this is the end. How is Israel to be a blessing to the nations now? How is God going to bring his promised blessing now?

There is nothing left.

Or is there?

The people aren't dead, at least, not all of them. Do you think God will abandon them completely? Or does he still have a plan for them?

Prayer: When it feels like the end of all things, Father God, are you still with us? Where are you in our brokenness, and our grief? Will we find you there, when it feels like all hope has been lost? God who has pity on your people, and on your dwelling place, who sends messengers over and over again, help us to hear you and turn our hearts toward you.

DECEMBER 19

The New Covenant

"The time is coming," declares the LORD, "when I will make a new covenant with the house of Israel and with the house of Judah. 32 It will not be like the covenant I made with their forefathers when I took them by the hand to lead them out of Egypt, because they broke my covenant, though I was a husband to them, " declares the LORD. 33 "This is the covenant I will make with the house of Israel after that time," declares the LORD. **"I will put my law in their minds and write it on their hearts. I will be their God, and they will be my people.** 34 No longer will a man teach his neighbor, or a man his brother, saying, 'Know the LORD,' because **they will all know me, from the least of them to the greatest," declares the LORD. "For I will forgive their wickedness and will remember their sins no more.**" (Jeremiah 31:31-34 NASB)

this is what the LORD, the God of Israel, says: 37 I will surely gather them from all the lands where I banish them in my furious anger and great wrath; I will bring them back to this place and let them live in safety. 38 They will be my people, and I will be their God. 39 **I will give them singleness of heart and action,** so that they will always fear me for their own good and the good of their children after them. 40 **I will make an everlasting covenant with them: I will never stop doing good to them,** and I will inspire them to fear me, so that they will never turn away from me. (Jeremiah 32:37-40 NASB)

14 " 'The days are coming,' declares the LORD, 'when **I will fulfill the gracious promise I made to the house of Israel and to the house of Judah. 15 "** **'In those days and at that time I will make a righteous Branch sprout from David's line; he will do what is just and right in the land.** 16 In those days Judah will be saved and Jerusalem will live in safety. This is the name by which it will be called: The LORD Our Righteousness.' 17 For this is what the LORD says: 'David will never fail to have a man to sit on the throne of the house of Israel, 18 nor will the priests, who are Levites, ever fail to have a man to stand before me continually to offer burnt offerings, to burn grain offerings and to present sacrifices.' " (Jeremiah 33:14-18 NASB)

In the years leading up to Israel's ruin, and their captivity in Babylon, God sent them prophets, many of them, to warn them, and to try and help them see what they were doing wrong so they could change in time.

Not many listened to them. Jeremiah was told by God to tell the King of Judah that destruction was coming. The king didn't like that much, so he had Jeremiah arrested instead of turning back to God.

But among all of the terrible things God gave Jeremiah to say, all of the dire predictions about the coming destruction, all of which came to pass, he also gave him these words of comfort.

Here are promises that God made to his people, in the time before they went back into exile, about a time when he would bring them back to the land he gave to their forefathers, and when he would make a new covenant with them.

He would write his law in their hearts and minds. They would know God personally and not need anyone else, prophet or otherwise, to tell them what God wanted, they would just know. He would give them singleness of heart and action, so that the things they want to do, to obey, to keep God's laws, they would now have the strength to do them.

Does it remind you of anything?

When was the last time people had God's law in their hearts, and just knew God?

How about in the Garden of Eden, with Adam and Eve, when they had the Breath of Life in them?

God has promised to forgive all their sin and forget their wickedness. It would be the same as it had been in the beginning. Maybe even better.

Some people in Babylon remembered these promises, and held onto them. They looked long and hard for evidence of God's forgiveness, and his breath, or spirit, (the words are almost exactly the same in Hebrew) coming back to them.

Several hundred years after Jeremiah there would still be people looking for the evidence of God's forgiveness. They would find it in the most unexpected of places, and in the most unexpected of ways.

Prayer: God who forgives, thank you that you have always wanted to forgive us, to make us more like you, to be so close to us that we know your law in our own hearts and minds. Thank you for the hope and comfort you give when all seems hopeless. You spoke to your people after all had been lost. You spoke to them words of comfort and hope. Speak also to our hearts words of comfort and hope when we feel that all has been lost. Help us to find you when we feel that we are lost in foreign lands far from home.

DECEMBER 20

Return to the Land

1 In the first year of Cyrus king of Persia, in order to fulfill the word of the LORD spoken by Jeremiah, the LORD moved the heart of Cyrus king of Persia to make a proclamation throughout his realm and to put it in writing: 2 "This is what Cyrus king of Persia says: " 'The LORD, the God of heaven, has given me all the kingdoms of the earth and he has appointed me to build a temple for him at Jerusalem in Judah. 3 Anyone of his people among you--may his God be with him, and let him go up to Jerusalem in Judah and build the temple of the LORD, the God of Israel, the God who is in Jerusalem. 4 And the people of any place where survivors may now be living are to provide him with silver and gold, with goods and livestock, and with freewill offerings for the temple of God in Jerusalem.' " 5 Then the family heads of Judah and Benjamin, and the priests and Levites--everyone whose heart God had moved--prepared to go up and build the house of the LORD in Jerusalem. 6 All their neighbors assisted them with articles of silver and gold, with goods and livestock, and with valuable gifts, in addition to all the freewill offerings. 7 Moreover, King Cyrus brought out the articles belonging to the temple of the LORD, which Nebuchadnezzar had carried away from Jerusalem and had placed in the temple of his god." (Ezra 1:1-7)

God kept his promise. The first part of it anyway. After 70 years the exiles were allowed to return home.

Not everyone chose to return though. Many, many people stayed in Babylon. They were comfortable there. They had good lives now. They didn't want to return to a ruined city and rebuild it. They didn't want to rebuild the temple of God.

But a remnant returned. God moved the people who had been faithful to him while they were gone to return.

That in itself is amazing! Think about it. The most of the time Israel was in the land they worshiped other gods and disobeyed God's rules. But during the exile there were many stories of people who remained faithful to God, and trusted him and refused to worship the God's of Babylon and Persia. There were people who loved God and wanted to be faithful.

Those people went back to the land once they could.

They rebuilt the temple, and the wall. They settled there with their families. They worked hard to keep all God's laws.

They settled in to wait for the rest of the promise. They waited and watched for the sign of God's forgiveness to come. They looked for the sign of God's blessing, God's presence. They dedicated the temple. Nothing happened. Well, no cloud of smoke and pillar of fire like when they had dedicated the first temple.

Still they waited.

When would God come to live with them again, to show them they were forgiven, and bring the promise to write his law on their hearts and make them his people again?

They would wait hundreds of years.

Do you know what the sign will be?

Prayer: God who restores, thank you that you keep your promises. Thank you that you gather us under your wings, that you bring your scattered children back to you and shelter us. Help us to be faithful as you are faithful. Help us to wait patiently to see your goodness, to have courage in our hearts as we wait for you.

DECEMBER 21

The Son of God

26 In the sixth month, God sent the angel Gabriel to Nazareth, a town in Galilee, 27 to a virgin pledged to be married to a man named Joseph, a descendant of David. The virgin's name was Mary. 28 The angel went to her and said, "Greetings, you who are highly favored! The Lord is with you." 29 Mary was greatly troubled at his words and wondered what kind of greeting this might be. 30 But the angel said to her, "Do not be afraid, Mary, you have found favor with God. 31 You will be with child and give birth to a son, and you are to give him the name Jesus. 32 He will be great and will be called the Son of the Most High. The Lord God will give him the throne of his father David, 33 and he will reign over the house of Jacob forever; his kingdom will never end." 34 "How will this be," Mary asked the angel, "since I am a virgin?" 35 The angel answered, "The Holy Spirit will come upon you, and the power of the Most High will overshadow you. So the holy one to be born will be called the Son of God. 36 Even Elizabeth your relative is going to have a child in her old age, and she who was said to be barren is in her sixth month. 37 For nothing is impossible with God." 38 "I am the Lord's servant," Mary answered. "May it be to me as you have said." Then the angel left her. (Luke 1:26-38)

Considering all the other babies in this long story of God's, perhaps it isn't that much of a surprise that this part also involves a baby.

* * *

But the people of Israel were looking for a warrior king, someone to rule over them and lead them into battles. They were looking for the kind of king they had had before. Even though God had promised them a better king.

They were also looking for someone who would free them from the Romans. For Israel was part of the Roman empire now. They paid taxes to the Roman ruler, soldiers were everywhere, watching for signs of rebellion, and punishing those who tried to make trouble. Israel may have been hoping that the sign of God's forgiveness looked more like a warrior to lead a rebellion and drive Rome out than anything else.

But the angel came to a poor girl, named Mary, a descendant of King David, who was to be married to a descendant of King David. The kings in Israel that Rome set up were not the descendants of David's line. They were there to make it look like Israel was freer than it was, and to help Rome keep the people in line.

The angel tells her she will become pregnant with the Son of God, and that God will give this child the throne of his father David, and he would rule over all of Israel forever and ever.

Imagine if you were Mary, and an angel just told you that

1. You would get pregnant before being married.
2. Your baby would be the son of God.
3. Your baby would be the true King of Israel, the heir of David.
4. His kingdom would never end.

Those are some pretty fantastic things to believe.

I wonder how she felt. What do you think?

In the end, she simply said, "May it be."

She probably knew how much this baby would upset her plans and change her life. But she believed the promises, and said yes anyway.
* * *

What would you have done?

Later on Mary says some things that show that she was strong woman who looked for God's justice in a world filled with darkness. Have you heard them before?

Mary said:
"My soul exalts the Lord,
[47] And my spirit has rejoiced in God my Savior.
[48] "For He has had regard for the humble state of His bondslave;
For behold, from this time on all generations will count me blessed.
[49] "For the Mighty One has done great things for me;
And holy is His name.
[50] "And His mercy is upon generation after generation
Toward those who fear Him.
[51] "He has done mighty deeds with His arm;
He has scattered *those who were* proud in the thoughts of their heart.
[52] "He has brought down rulers from *their* thrones,
And has exalted those who were humble.
[53] "He has filled the hungry with good things;
And sent away the rich empty-handed.
[54] "He has given help to Israel His servant,
 In remembrance of His mercy,
[55] As He spoke to our fathers,
To Abraham and his descendants forever." (Luke 1:46-55)

After years of waiting, the true king is about to arrive, and it's not what anyone expected it to be.

Prayer: God who does great things, who fills the hungry with good things and shows mercy to those who trust, obey and reverence you, thank you for your mercy. Thank you for a plan so much bigger than kingdoms of earth, and revolutions. Thank you that your plan extended to redeeming everyone, everywhere. That your plan was much greater than we could possibly imagine. Help us to believe in your promises, and to say yes to your calling, even if it will change our lives forever when we do.

DECEMBER 22

God With Us

18 This is how the birth of Jesus Christ came about: His mother Mary was pledged to be married to Joseph, but before they came together, she was found to be with child through the Holy Spirit. 19 Because Joseph her husband was a righteous man and did not want to expose her to public disgrace, he had in mind to divorce her quietly. 20 But after he had considered this, an angel of the Lord appeared to him in a dream and said, "Joseph son of David, do not be afraid to take Mary home as your wife, because what is conceived in her is from the Holy Spirit. 21 She will give birth to a son, and you are to give him the name Jesus, because he will save his people from their sins." 22 All this took place to fulfill what the Lord had said through the prophet: 23 "The virgin will be with child and will give birth to a son, and they will call him Immanuel"--which means, "God with us." 24 When Joseph woke up, he did what the angel of the Lord had commanded him and took Mary home as his wife. 25 But he had no union with her until she gave birth to a son. And he gave him the name Jesus. (Matthew 1:18-25)

Imagine poor Joseph. You are getting ready to marry a girl and you find out that she is pregnant, with somebody else's baby.

It looked bad for Mary. It looked like she had broken her promises to Joseph. Girls like her, who broke their marriage promises, were often killed.

Joseph didn't want anyone to hurt Mary. He didn't want to be her husband anymore either, but he didn't want to accuse her and have everyone hurt her and throw stones at her.

He was trying to find a kind way to deal with this uncomfortable situation that freed him from his promises to Mary, since she hadn't kept her promises to him, but that kept her from getting hurt.

He wanted to act rightly, according to God's law, which is what it means to be righteous.

Then he had a dream, and all that changed.

"Don't be afraid to take Mary as your wife."

Why do you think he would be afraid?

Well, if Mary was already pregnant, before they were properly married, and he married her anyway, everyone would thing that he broke his promises too, and did something dishonorable. They would think he had disrespected her, and himself. He would lose a lot of respect, from his friends, his family, and his community.

Not only that, imagine being the guy who is raising the child who is from God and who will save his people from their sins. That's a lot of pressure.

But Joseph believed the angel, he trusted God that this child was a sign that God was with his people again, and he took Mary as his wife. He protected her and the baby and cared for them

Do you think you could be as brave as Joseph was?

Prayer: God who is with us, thank you that you know what it is to be human. You know what it is to be afraid. You understand our weakness and you help us in our fear. You meet us, and you tell us to not be afraid. Help us to be brave. Help us to trust you. Help us to live our lives worried most about what you think of us, and not afraid of what others think.

DECEMBER 23

For All Nations

5 And now the LORD says-- he who formed me in the womb to be his servant to **bring Jacob back to him and gather Israel to himself**, for I am honored in the eyes of the LORD and my God has been my strength-- 6 he says: "It is too small a thing for you to be my servant to restore the tribes of Jacob and bring back those of Israel I have kept. **I will also make you a light for the Gentiles, that you may bring my salvation to the ends of the earth.**" 7 This is what the LORD says-- the Redeemer and Holy One of Israel-- to him who was despised and abhorred by the nation, to the servant of rulers: **"Kings will see you and rise up, princes will see and bow down**, because of the LORD, who is faithful, the Holy One of Israel, who has chosen you." (Isaiah 49:5-7 NASB)

Magi from the east came to Jerusalem 2 and asked, **"Where is the one who has been born king of the Jews? We saw his star in the east and have come to worship him."** 3 When King Herod heard this he was disturbed, and all Jerusalem with him. 4 When he had called together all the people's chief priests and teachers of the law, he asked them where the Christ was to be born. 5 "In Bethlehem in Judea," they replied, "for this is what the prophet has written: 6 " 'But you, Bethlehem, in the land of Judah, are by no means least among the rulers of Judah; for out of you will come a ruler who will be the shepherd of my people Israel.' " (Matthew 2:1b-6 NASB)

The people of Israel have been waiting for the sign of God's forgiveness. Perhaps that's why Joseph, as we read yesterday, was able to believe the angel in his dream about the baby in Mary's belly. The angel said he would "Save his people from their sins."

But Israel has only been thinking of themselves. Remember back when we read about how Israel was supposed to be a nation of priests, who would show the rest of the world what God was like? Well, since they returned from exile they have been thinking mostly about how to be free to rule themselves the way they like and not be burdened by all these other nations who won't leave them alone. Being a light to the nations is the farthest thing from their minds.

But when the prophet Isaiah was talking about the coming redemption, after exile, that's one of the main things he talks about. He talks about Israel being the place the other nations come to meet with God.

God's salvation, his new promises to Israel that he has made aren't just for them, they are for everyone, to the ends of the earth.

And now, as Israel's redeemer is born to Mary and Joseph, far from any palace. When his birth goes almost completely unnoticed by almost everyone in Israel, Magi, gentiles from the East, see a sign in the heavens and make the long journey to see the one who will bring salvation to the whole earth.

God's salvation, it was always for everyone. When Israel didn't show the earth the light of God, he came himself, as a little tiny baby, to get the job done. The light of the world was contained in the body of a girl, making a long journey, to a place foretold by prophets hundreds and hundreds of years ago, all the way back to Jacob as he lay dying and gave Joseph's son Ephraim the greater blessing, even though he was younger. For Bethlehem is in Ephraim, the land settled by Ephraim's descendants and named after him, after their tribe.

All those promises, all those prophecies are looking forward to this moment, this child, and what he will do when he becomes a man.

Do you know who he is yet?

* * *

Do you know what it is he did?

Prayer: God who forgives, thank you that your forgiveness extends to all people, in every nation. Thank you that while you started with Israel, you have always wanted to bring all the earth into your family. Thank you for light in the darkness, for saving all of us, everywhere, for all time. Help us to be the light to the world that you created us to be, to shine your hope so that those who are lost and hopeless can see your salvation, and come to you for forgiveness and hope.

DECEMBER 24

Great Joy, For All People

1 In those days Caesar Augustus issued a decree that a census should be taken of the entire Roman world. 2 (This was the first census that took place while Quirinius was governor of Syria.) 3 And everyone went to his own town to register. 4 So Joseph also went up from the town of Nazareth in Galilee to Judea, to Bethlehem the town of David, because he belonged to the house and line of David. 5 He went there to register with Mary, who was pledged to be married to him and was expecting a child. 6 While they were there, the time came for the baby to be born, 7 and she gave birth to her firstborn, a son. She wrapped him in cloths and placed him in a manger, because there was no room for them in the inn.

8 And there were shepherds living out in the fields nearby, keeping watch over their flocks at night. 9 An angel of the Lord appeared to them, and the glory of the Lord shone around them, and they were terrified. 10 But the angel said to them, "Do not be afraid. I bring you good news of great joy that will be for all the people. 11 Today in the town of David a Savior has been born to you; he is Christ the Lord. 12 This will be a sign to you: You will find a baby wrapped in cloths and lying in a manger." 13 Suddenly a great company of the heavenly host appeared with the angel, praising God and saying, 14 "Glory to God in the highest, and on earth peace to men on whom his favor rests." 15 When the angels had left them and

gone into heaven, the shepherds said to one another, "Let's go to Bethlehem and see this thing that has happened, which the Lord has told us about." 16 So they hurried off and found Mary and Joseph, and the baby, who was lying in the manger. 17 When they had seen him, they spread the word concerning what had been told them about this child, 18 and all who heard it were amazed at what the shepherds said to them. 19 But Mary treasured up all these things and pondered them in her heart. 20 The shepherds returned, glorifying and praising God for all the things they had heard and seen, which were just as they had been told. (Luke 2:1-20 NASB)

Joseph and Mary traveled all the way to Bethlehem, Mary heavy with child. They probably walked the whole way. Maybe there was a donkey. The Bible doesn't say. But because of the decree of a Roman ruler, who also ruled over Israel, they were forced to make the long journey to the land of their ancestors. The town of David, the king of Israel, the land settled by Ephraim, great, great-grandson of Abraham, the home of Ruth and Boaz. They were forced to come here, the place all the promises had spoken of, for the promised child to be born.

They didn't have anywhere fancy to stay. There wasn't room for them in an inn or house. They stayed where the animals stayed. The great king who would draw all of the world back to God, would bring forgiveness of sins to his people, who was the light of the world, his first bed was a feeding trough for animals.

God, who always told Israel how much he cared about the poor, came as a poor child, to poor parents.

The first people he told about his coming were not kings, not rulers, not anyone important at all. They were shepherds. Men staying out in the dark taking care of their flocks, just as Abraham, Isaac, and Jacob had done, long ago.

But these shepherds were also descendants of Abraham. Do you think they knew about the promises, to Abraham and his descendants, the promises to them?

* * *

They probably did. They would have understood the importance of a baby being born in the town of David, the king. They would have known what all that meant.

They were terrified when they saw the angel, but the angel told them that he brought "Good news, of great joy, for all people." Not just important people, not even just the descendants of Abraham, but for all people. A savior has been born. The promise has been fulfilled. God is once again living with his people!

This child Jesus will grow up and be the promised blessing to the entire world.

Do you know how?

Prayer: God of the poor, who doesn't care about things like wealth or status, thank you that you came to us, to all of us. Thank you that you loved us so much that you became one of us, in order to act our your forgiveness and redemption in our history, in our story. Help us to receive you with joy. Help us to welcome in those whom you love. Help us to be part of the blessing that you bring to the world.

DECEMBER 25

God Comes to His Temple Again

21 On the eighth day, when it was time to circumcise him, he was named Jesus, the name the angel had given him before he had been conceived. 22 When the time of their purification according to the Law of Moses had been completed, Joseph and Mary took him to Jerusalem to present him to the Lord 23 (as it is written in the Law of the Lord, "Every firstborn male is to be consecrated to the Lord"), 24 and to offer a sacrifice in keeping with what is said in the Law of the Lord: "a pair of doves or two young pigeons." 25 Now there was a man in Jerusalem called Simeon, who was righteous and devout. **He was waiting for the consolation of Israel, and the Holy Spirit was upon him.** 26 It had been revealed to him by the Holy Spirit that he would not die before he had seen the Lord's Christ. 27 Moved by the Spirit, he went into the temple courts. When the parents brought in the child Jesus to do for him what the custom of the Law required, 28 Simeon took him in his arms and praised God, saying: 29 "Sovereign Lord, as you have promised, you now dismiss your servant in peace. 30 **For my eyes have seen your salvation, 31 which you have prepared in the sight of all people, 32 a light for revelation to the Gentiles and for glory to your people Israel.**" 33 The child's father and mother marveled at what was said about him. (Luke 2:21-33 NASB)

* * *

Remember when they rebuilt the temple of God in Jerusalem? The temple was supposed to be God's house, where he lived with his people, and they went to meet with him. Only, God hadn't been in his temple for almost 400 years.

Then Mary and Joseph take their baby son to the temple to dedicate him to God, he was probably between 1 and 2 months old, and Simeon, an old prophet who has been waiting to see the sign of God's forgiveness picks up the child and says, "At last. He is come. Now I can die in peace."

Hundreds of people were probably there that day. Only two of them noticed the salvation of God entering the temple. Simeon, and an old woman named Anna, also full of God's spirit. Those two noticed. Those two saw. Those two spent their days looking, and all their time listening to God.

God's promise was fulfilled. He lived with his people again.

All that most people that day saw was a little baby, with two very poor parents, coming through the temple as thousands had done before.

It's a lot different from the cloud and thunder and fire of the first time isn't it?

Why do you suppose that is?

Why did Jesus come in secret, so only those who were looking could see him?

Do you remember what God told the prophet Samuel, when he was looking at David's brothers and thinking they must be the ones God had chosen, since they were handsome. He said, "Man looks at the outward appearance, but the LORD looks at the heart."

God was after hearts. He always has been. I think that has something to do with it.

When Isaiah the prophet talked about the one who was to come, the promised deliverer, he said this. "1 Who has believed our message and to whom has the arm of the LORD been revealed? 2 He grew up before him like a tender shoot, and like a root out of dry ground. He had no beauty or majesty to attract us to him, nothing in his appearance that we should desire him. 3 He was despised and rejected by men, a man of sorrows, and familiar with suffering. Like one from whom men hide their faces he was despised, and we esteemed him not. 4 Surely he took up our infirmities and carried our sorrows, yet we considered him stricken by God, smitten by him, and afflicted." (Isaiah 53:1-4 NASB)

God came, and very few knew him, because their hearts were not looking for him. "9 *The true light that gives light to every man was coming into the world. 10 He was in the world, and though the world was made through him, the world did not recognize him. 11 He came to that which was his own, but his own did not receive him.*" (John 1:9-11 NASB)

But Jesus did what he came to do anyway. He kept the promise. He acted out God's forgiveness here, in the history of our world. And because of him, you, me, everyone can have the breath of Life in them again if they say yes to it. As always, it didn't look anything like they expected it to. Do you know what happened?

Is your heart looking for Jesus? Do you see where God is working all around you? Have you tried listening and watching to see?

Prayer: God who lives, in many times past you have lived with your people. In the wilderness you stayed with them in a pillar of fire and a pillar of cloud. In the temple that Solomon dedicated to you, you once again showed your presence in a great cloud that filled the inner sanctuary. You keep your promise to enter the new temple again, and dwell with your people. But this time you came as one of us, in skin and bone, humble and small. Later you sent your spirit to dwell in each one of us, living with us in our very hearts. Help us to turn our hearts to you, to always be looking for you. Help us to recognize you Jesus when we see you at work.

EXTRA READINGS FOR ADVENT SUNDAYS

The Advent Candles and Wreath

[This section includes a guide and ideas for observing the candle lighting part of advent as well as readings to go with each candle.]

Many branches of Christian tradition and practice include lighting the Advent candles on the 4 Sundays that lead up Christmas. Often these candles are arranged in a wreath of greenery as well. The evergreen circle symbolizes the love of God. It has no beginning, and no end, and the evergreen branches don't fade, even in winter.

Some Christian traditions have specific colors for each candle. My Catholic friends light 3 purple candles, and one pink candle, placed in a beautiful wreath that they light at dinner time each night of advent. My Norwegian friends light a row of pure white candles every morning before sunrise.

One year, just after our family moved to Thailand, I didn't have any pretty wreaths or candle holders. We took tin cans from the recycling and using a hammer and nails banged holes into the sides of them that formed the words: love, hope, peace, and joy. We put small tea light candles in those cans and lined them up on our table for the month of December.

Your advent candles don't have to be fancy, or beautiful, or "right". There is wonder in simply remembering through lighting these tiny flames how hope shines bright in the darkness, as we wait for the promises of God to be fulfilled.

If you want to do it, just start with what you have. It will be enough.

* * *

On the first Sunday of Advent, you will light one candle. If you like, you can continue to light this candle all week long. (You'll have to replace it at some point. And make sure it's in a fire safe holder.) Many people keep their advent candles on their dining room table and light them during their evening meal.

On the Second Sunday of Advent, you begin with the first candle already lit. Then you light the second candle. This pattern continues with the third and fourth candles as well, until all the candles are lit.

Some people keep a 5th Christ candle in the center, and they light this candle, in addition to all the other candles, on Christmas Eve.

When my children were small we would gather near the advent wreath and turn out all the lights. In the dark we would sing the first verse of "Oh Come Emmanuel" and then we would light the first hope candle and see how the tiny flame broke through the darkness.

Each Sunday as we added more light we could experience how the light was growing, and how each tiny light makes the room brighter. (We would also add another verse of the song.) It's a lovely metaphor for how the light of God's kingdom grows as we each add our own light to it.

We don't do a lot of Christmas decorating at the beginning of December. I like to keep the main focus on the wreath and the candles. As each week goes by we add a few more decorations, gradually increasing the festive feeling in the house as the number of candles increase. Advent is primarily a season of waiting, not yet of celebration. The celebration comes when Christ comes on Christmas Eve, and Christmas Day.

This might be a different way of thinking about the days of December than you normally do, but I encourage you to try it. Don't jump ahead to the celebration right away. Take some time to sit with the longing, with the way this world groans for the fulfillment of all of God's promises.

Let the advent readings encourage you that God keeps his promises, and is still at work to make all things right, even now. Especially now.

The First Sunday of Advent - Hope

To begin: Turn out all the lights in the room and sit in darkness for a moment. If you like, sing "oh Come Emmanuel" in the dark. Take a moment to notice together how hard it is to see, or do anything when it it dark.

Now light the first candle and read together. (On this day you will light only one candle.) You may wish to keep this candle lit all week, especially if you have placed your candles in a central place, such as a dinner table. Many families light the advent candles in their wreath at every evening meal they are at home for during the advent season. For the first week of advent you will continue to light only one candle.

Reading:

> 2 "The people who walk in darkness
> Will see a great light;
> Those who live in a dark land,
> The light will shine on them.
> 3 You will multiply the nation,
> You will increase their joy;
> They will rejoice in Your presence"
> (Isaiah 9:2-3 NASB)

Additional reading: John 1:1-5

On the first Sunday of advent we light the candle of hope. We notice how a tiny flame shines big in the darkness and makes it so that we can see and do things that we cannot do when we are caught in the darkness with no light.

We remember together that God made big promises and we hold onto the hope that God will keep his promises to us and to all people.

We come to the season of advent knowing that there are many things in the world that are in darkness, that are broken, and need God's light and healing touch. We kindle the hope that comes from trusting in God's promises and believing that He isn't finished yet. God is at work healing and redeeming and making the world whole. We wait and watch the light, hoping in his promises, knowing that we are in the middle of the story right now, and God isn't finished yet.

Prayer: God of Light, remember us. Thank you that you promised to make all things new, that your light shines on in the darkness, and the darkness has not ever overcome the light. Help us to trust in you. Help us to hope in you, to wait patiently for your promises, even when we don't see how you could possibly fix or make whole the broken things we see in the world. Help us to trust that you are always at work, and that there is always hope because of you.

13 I would have lost heart, unless I had believed
That I would see the goodness of the Lord
In the land of the living.

* * *

14 Wait on the Lord;
Be of good courage,
And He shall strengthen your heart;
Wait, I say, on the Lord!
(Psalm 27:13-14NKJV)

The Second Sunday of Advent - Peace

Begin: Start with one candle already lit. Sing together "oh Come Emmanuel," if you choose.

Light the second candle and then read together.

Reading:

> 6 For a Child will be born to us, a Son will be given to us;
> And the government will rest on His shoulders;
> And His name will be called Wonderful Counselor, Mighty God,
> Eternal Father, Prince of Peace.
> 7 There will be no end to the increase of His government or of peace
> On the throne of David and over his kingdom,
> To establish it and to uphold it with justice and righteousness
> From then on and forevermore.
> The zeal of the Lord of armies will accomplish this.
> (Isaiah 9:6-7NASB)

Somewhere in the world, right now, people are fighting with each other. A brother and a sister are arguing over a toy. A man and a woman are shouting at each other because they are angry, and maybe because they feel like the other person doesn't really care about them. Armies are fighting with guns, and bombs, and tanks. Countries fight countries. Militias fight militias. Some people fight because they believe their cause is just, and that if they don't fight, they will allow evil and unjust people to have power over many innocent people. Some people fight because they want money and power.

Whatever the reasons, the world is not at peace.

* * *

But we all long for peace. We long for there to be no more fighting, in our homes, our schools, our countries. The world longs for peace.

What is amazing to me though is that there isn't as much fighting as you might expect. Given how many people there are in the world, the number of people fighting each other is actually very small. Not only that, many of the people who argue find a way to make peace with each other very quickly. They decide to not hold a grudge, to move on, to forgive.

Part of why there isn't as much fighting as there might be is because of the laws and the courts that many countries have.

The prophet Isaiah recognizes that peace is linked to justice and righteousness. For there to be true peace, there must be justice. Justice is where things are right, things are decided fairly, where people trust that those in charge will make rules that benefit them and protect them.

Righteousness is being right according to God's law. The king that God promises through the prophet Isaiah is one who will uphold God's law, who will establish a kingdom that is good and just. It will be a place where the powerful don't take advantage of the weak and where everyone is cared for and has what they need. Everyone will trust that the king will act according to God's good law, and always do what is right.

When this king comes, there will be true peace, and it will not end.

Prayer: God of peace, thank you that you promised to bring peace. Thank you that the day will coming when your perfect peace will reign over all the earth and all will trust in the righteous king who will establish it. Help us to seek peace in our own lives with those around us. Help us to act with justice and mercy toward those around us. Help us to forgive those who have wronged us and look for ways to be at peace with them. Help us to learn what your justice and righteousness look like in our daily lives.

The Third Sunday of Advent - Joy

Begin with 2 candles already lit. If your advent candles have a 3 purples candles and one pink candle, today is when you light the pink candle. In many church traditions purple is the color of sacrifice, preparation, and even penance. Advent is a time of waiting, of longing, of experiencing and living through the story of a world waiting for a savior. Purple is a color that represents all of that. However, we can't light a purple sacrifice candle on a day of joy. Pink is the color of rejoicing in this tradition. So the candle for the Advent Sunday of Joy is pink instead of purple.

[Note: Often on this Sunday we read of the shepherds in the fields hearing the news of great joy about the birth of Jesus. Since the advent readings in this book have that story in a different place, I have not put that reading here.]

Reading:

> 1 The Spirit of the Lord God is upon me,
> Because the Lord anointed me
> To bring good news to the humble;
> He has sent me to bind up the brokenhearted,
> To proclaim release to captives
> And freedom to prisoners;
> 2 To proclaim the favorable year of the Lord
> And the day of vengeance of our God;
> **To comfort all who mourn,**
> **3 To grant those who mourn in Zion,**
> **Giving them a garland instead of ashes,**
> **The oil of gladness instead of mourning,**

The cloak of praise instead of a disheartened spirit.
So they will be called oaks of righteousness,
The planting of the Lord, that He may be glorified.
4 Then they will rebuild the ancient ruins,
They will raise up the former devastations;
And they will repair the ruined cities,
The desolations of many generations.
5 Strangers will stand and pasture your flocks,
And foreigners will be your farmers and your vinedressers.
6 **But you will be called the priests of the Lord;**
You will be spoken of as ministers of our God.
You will eat the wealth of nations,
And you will boast in their riches.
7 Instead of your shame you will have a double portion,
And instead of humiliation they will shout for joy over their portion.
Therefore they will possess a double portion in their land,
Everlasting joy will be theirs.

10 **I will rejoice greatly in the Lord,**
My soul will be joyful in my God;
For He has clothed me with garments of salvation,
He has wrapped me with a robe of righteousness,
Isaiah 61:1-7, 10[NASB}

God promises joy! He promises his people that he will give them joy. After years and years of mourning, God will give them joy.

Again we see God's promise to redeem his people. God promises to restore everything that was lost, to give gladness instead of mourning, to repair what was broken and torn down, to make his people into his priests, the people who show the world what God is like, who bring others into the presence of God.

This promise was given to God's people in the middle of their exile in Babylon, when their country had been completely destroyed and many of their people carried off into captivity. They have lost everything. They are strangers in a strange land, captured and carried off, taken from their homeland. But God promises them joy.

God still promises joy. God promises that He will make all things right in the end and that He is at work making stories that feel utterly hopeless into stories that have joyful endings. Only God can do that.

Do you have anything that feels hopeless in your life right now? Do you have any big sad things that you feel will never stop being sad?

What would happen if you trusted God with your sad thing, and gave it to Him? What if you offered your mourning to God and ask him if he can turn it into joy?

You never know what God can do with something. He is the one who restores everything in the end.

Prayer: God of joy, giver of life and restoration, thank you that you are with us in the middle of our mourning. Thank you that you speak words of comfort to us when we are lost and afraid and sad. Thank you that when things feel like they are at their worst, you are still there. Thank you that you don't leave us in the sad, lonely, and desolate places. Thank you that you lead us out of mourning, that you bring us into a good place, a place of rejoicing. Help us to know your presence with us as we mourn. Help us to feel your comfort. Help us to trust that joy will come, in your perfect time.

The Fourth Sunday of Advent - Love

Today you will light the 4th candle, beginning with the first 3 already lit. On Christmas Eve or Christmas Day you may wish to light the Christ candle, the fifth candle in the center of the wreath. You can use the reading for December 24th or 25th as you light the the Christ candle. Both will be appropriate.

Reading:

"For God so loved the world, that He gave His only Son, so that everyone who believes in Him will not perish, but have eternal life." John 3:16

And now we come to the ultimate reason for everything, love.

God loves us. God loves his creation. God loves the people He created. God does not leave His creation to suffer. Even when everything went terribly wrong and the people He created to be His presence here on the earth and complete His creation disobeyed Him and lost the breath of life and the power they needed to do God's will, God did not abandon them. God did not abandon us. God so loved that He took it upon himself to put His breath back in us, to fill all creation with His Spirit, to give us the power again to be His presence in the earth, His partners in completing the work of creation, of healing this world.

* * *

You and I get to be part of that every day that we choose to obey God, and we don't have to do it alone. Jesus came as one of us to accomplish God's mission to give us back the breath of life, to make us able to be God's representatives on the earth. Jesus was born to act out God's forgiveness in our history, and give us God's spirit.

The story isn't finished yet. The birth of Jesus is just the beginning. There is more to come. Jesus will accomplish God's plans for the earth, for us.

We remember that part of the story at a different time of year called Lent, and Easter. Advent is almost over. The waiting is almost over. God's promises are being fulfilled!

Prayer: God of love, who loves us completely and totally just as we are, who never abandoned us, never leaves us alone even when we fail and make mistakes, thank you for your love. Thank you that when we needed to be saved, from ourselves, from our own bad choices, you yourself came, became like us, and you yourself saved us. You are the only one who could have done it. You are the only one who could fulfill your own righteous requirements and save us from our own sin. Help us to receive your love in our own hearts and pass it on it to everyone around us. Help us to be part of your work to heal creation, to complete your plans on the earth for everything to be made right. Amen

AFTERWARD

Thank you for reading along this Advent.

These Advent readings don't tell the full story. They stop with the coming of Jesus into the temple as a child.

The story continues in the lead up to Easter and Resurrection Sunday.

I also have a series of Lent readings for your family that continues the story of how Jesus acted out God's forgiveness and redemption in history. If you enjoyed this series, I invite you to make those readings part of your Lent and Easter observances this coming year.

Reviews help people to know if this book is worth their time and money.

Please take a moment to leave a review of this book on Amazon so others can know the value they are getting in this little series of advent readings for their family.

Made in the USA
Las Vegas, NV
15 November 2024

11869140R00080